Folens Geography

An Indian Locality: Jodhpur in Rajasthan

Teacher Resource Guide

Steve and Patricia Harrison
Lynn and John Lancaster

Folens Publishers

Acknowledgements

The authors and publisher would like to thank the following for their permission to reproduce photographs and other material:

Jill Bennett	poster 2 — picture 10
	poster 3 — pictures 3–4, 8–9, 12–13
	poster 4 — pictures 6–7, 10–12, 14, 18
	poster 5 — pictures 4–6, 8–10, 12, 14, 16, 18–20
	photos 5–10, 13, 19–20
Robert Crowther	poster 1 — picture 1
CM Dixon	poster 2 — pictures 4, 6, 8–9
ET Archive	poster 2 — picture 3
Robert Harding	poster 2 — picture 5
Steve Harrison	poster 1 — pictures 4–6, 8, 10, 12–13, 15–16
Hutchinson	poster 1 — picture 9
Gwen Kebbell	poster 1 — picture 11
	poster 3 — picture 11
Janet Lancaster	poster 4 — picture 3
Rob Lancaster	cover
	poster 1 — pictures 2, 14
	poster 3 — pictures 1–2, 5–7, 10, 14–18
	poster 4 — pictures 1–2, 4–5, 8–9, 13, 15–17
	poster 5 — pictures 1–3, 11, 13, 15, 17
	photos 1–4, 11–12, 14–18
Still Pictures	poster 1 — picture 7
Zefa	poster 1 — picture 3

Folens allows photocopying of pages marked 'copiable page' for educational use, providing that this use is within the confines of the purchasing institution. Copiable pages should not be declared in any return in respect of any photocopying licence.

Folens books are protected by international copyright laws. All rights are reserved. The copyright of all materials in this book, except where otherwise stated, remains the property of the publisher and authors. No part of this publication may be reproduced, stored in a retrieval system, or transmitted, in any form or by any means, for whatever purpose, without the written permission of Folens Limited.

This resource may be used in a variety of ways. However, it is not intended that teachers or children should write directly into the book itself.

The authors hereby assert their moral rights to be identified as the authors of this work in accordance with the Copyright, Designs and Patents Act 1988.

Editor: Alison MacTier   Layout artist: Suzanne Ward   Cover design: John Hawkins

Illustrations: Julian Baker (posters), Gary Clifford – The Drawing Room (maps and diagrams in resource book); Virginia Gray – Graham-Cameron Illustration (poster 2, resource book), Tony O'Donnell (resource book).

© 1997 Folens Limited, on behalf of the authors.

Every effort has been made to contact copyright holders of material used in this book. If any have been overlooked, we will be pleased to make any necessary arrangements.

British Library Cataloguing in Publication Data. A catalogue record for this book is available from the British Library.

First published 1997 by Folens Limited, Dunstable and Dublin.

Folens Limited, Albert House, Apex Business Centre, Boscombe Road, Dunstable, LU5 4RL, England.

ISBN 1 85276 855–X

Printed in the UK.

Contents

Using Folens Geography	4
Using An Indian Locality	5

POSTERS AND PHOTOS
Using the photopack	6
Poster 1	
The Indian subcontinent	8
Poster 2	
Indus Valley civilisation	10
Poster 3	
Everyday life in Rajasthan	11
Poster 4	
Everyday life in Jodhpur	13
Poster 5	
Transport	14

HISTORY
Teacher page	
India time line	16
Teacher page	
The Indus civilisation – activities	18
Pupil information sheet 1	
The Indus Valley civilisation	19
Activity sheet 1	
Indus Valley artefacts	20
Activity sheet 2	
A city in the Indus Valley	21
Activity sheet 3	
Make your own Indus Valley seal	22
Activity sheet 4	
What happened to the people of the Indus Valley?	23

INDIA IN CONTEXT
Teacher page	
A snapshot of India	24
Activity sheet 5	
Travelling to India	25
Map 1	
A map of India	26
Map 2	
The landscape of India	27
Pupil information sheet 2	
Weather in India	28
Activity sheet 6	
Climate and weather	29
Activity sheet 7	
Weather: comparing capital cities	30
Activity sheet 8	
India's population	31
Map 3	
Train travel through Rajasthan	32
Activity sheet 9	
Train travel	33
Pupil information sheet 3	
Industries in India	34
Activity sheet 10	
Trade and industry	35
Pupil information sheet 4	
Religion in India	36

RAJASTHAN
Teacher page	
Rajasthan – background information	37
Activity sheet 11	
Rajasthan – map work	38
Activity sheet 12	
The physical features of Rajasthan	39
Pupil information sheet 5	
On holiday in Rajasthan	40
Activity sheet 13	
On holiday in Rajasthan	41
Activity sheet 14	
A tourist in Rajasthan	42
Map 4	
A tourist in Rajasthan	43
Teacher page	
Farming	44
Activity sheet 15	
Life in rural Rajasthan	45
Pupil information sheet 6	
Deserts	46
Activity sheet 16	
Desert life in Rajasthan	47
Activity sheet 17	
Protecting the environment	48
Activity sheet 18	
Tourism	49

JODHPUR
Teacher page	
An introduction to Jodhpur	50
Activity sheet 19	
The streets of Jodhpur	51
Map 5	
A map of Jodhpur	52
Activity sheet 20	
Finding your way around Jodhpur	53
Activity sheet 21	
Origins of Jodhpur	54
Activity sheet 22	
Meherangarh Fort	55
Pupil information sheet 7	
A day in the life of TulsiRam Jat	56
Pupil information sheet 8	
Children in Jodhpur	57
Activity sheet 23	
At school in Jodhpur	58
Pupil information sheet 9	
Living in Jodhpur	59
Teacher page	
Living in Jodhpur – activities	60
Activity sheet 24	
The puppet makers of Jodhpur	61
Teacher page	
Reviewing the topic	62
Teacher page	
Something to cook	64

Using Folens Geography

Folens Geography is a comprehensive teaching and learning programme for pupils aged four to twelve.

Big Book 1

Format
- 420mm x 600mm
- Colour artwork
- Central wiro spine
- Every page is laminated

Key features
- *Folens Geography* aims to develop children's geographical understanding by starting from familiar stories, rhymes and activities.
- Lamination allows children to use water-based pens.

Big Book 2

Format
- 420mm x 600mm
- Colour photos and maps
- Central wiro spine
- Laminated pages

Key features
- The photos introduce real places into geography. They include oblique aerial photos, a satellite photo of the world and a world map.
- Many places on the map are illustrated by photos.

Teacher Resource Guides

Each Big Book is accompanied by a colour Teacher Resource Guide, featuring:
- photocopiable activity pages with cross-curricular links
- stories and poems with key geographical activities and language
- resources for the teacher to develop into geographical games.

Locality Packs

An Indian Locality

Format
- large tourist map of Rajasthan
- 5 A1 colour posters
- 20 A4 colour photos
- 64-page Teacher Resource Guide

Key features
The locality pack provides:
- ideas to integrate history and geography
- maps at a variety of scales
- photographs and artwork
- data
- historical background information
- geographical background information.

Skills are developed through:
- map and plan interpretation
- using photographic evidence
- tasks requiring atlas skills
- use of appropriate geographical vocabulary.

Other locality packs

An Egyptian Locality
This material is designed for an integrated history–geography topic linking Ancient Egypt and life in contemporary Luxor.

A Greek Locality
This material is designed for integrated history and geography topic work linking Ancient Greece and life in contemporary Epidavros.

A Rural Locality
Sedbergh in the Yorkshire Dales offers the opportunity to study a rural upland settlement.

An Urban Locality
The study of Clerkenwell, a suburb of London, demonstrates typical urban features relating to people, places and industry.

Using An Indian Locality

Curriculum changes in recent years have tended to lead to a somewhat over-compartmentalised curriculum. This has not always been to the advantage of children as it can lead to a fragmented curriculum.

In this locality pack we have sought to draw together the historical and the geographical. The region of India chosen is where the Indus Valley civilisation once flourished. The contemporary study of this region deals with a number of settlements but focuses particularly on Jodhpur.

Those schools wishing to carry out a locality study that provides a contrast with their own locality will find substantial material within this pack for such an approach. As an Indian locality, Jodhpur meets the locational requirements of the geography curriculum while Rajasthan and its Indus Valley past is an appropriate unit of study in history.

The Indian subcontinent was subject to partition in 1947 creating the modern states of Pakistan and India whose shared border runs through the lands which once formed the Indus Valley civilisation.

Key themes

The key themes of geography are embraced within this pack. **Settlement** is studied through material on the various cities of Rajasthan. Udaipur, Jaipur and Jodhpur are all featured, allowing contrast within India as well as between India and the UK.

The **weather** is a major factor for any study of India. Its effect on jobs, landscape, farming, building style and tourism are all included.

Environmental change addresses how people affect the environment in Rajasthan, for example through the construction of the great canal system designed to 'green' the desert, the over-grazing of animals leading to desertification, the population growth which places pressure on the environment and the need to sustain ancient monuments which act as a magnet for tourists.

We have tried to approach the linking of history and geography in a way which reflects the importance of culture and religion on people's past and present practices. Just as physical geography contributed to the development of Rajasthan's military past, so today much of the region's society and economy is shaped by its history.

Each poster and photo corresponds to notes in this book that provide background information and suggestions for using the images. This is further developed through activity sheets that require the use of resources such as photos, artwork, maps and data.

Finally it is important to help the children understand the enormous period of time which has elapsed since the Indus Valley civilisation thrived. The Indus Valley cities of Harappa and Mohenjo-daro are broadly contemporary with the building of the Great Pyramids in Egypt. The time period from the building of the city of Mohenjo-daro to the birth of Christ is greater than the period from that birth to the present day.

Using the photopack

Photo	Purpose	Links
HOMES 1 Village home.	A large number of people in Rajasthan live in rural localities – small villages or clusters of houses. Here is a typical village home in the Thar Desert. Notice the pots stacked outside for collecting water, cooking and so on.	• Use with activity sheets 8, 15 and 16 on population, rural and desert life. • Page 44 contains background information on farming.

2 Town homes:
  a Traditional
  b Modern.
	These are increasingly being made from concrete – the cement industry is growing in Rajasthan. The other is made from wood construction. Notice the flat roofs – children can discuss reasons for this style, and compare with their own homes.	• Use with activity sheets 15 and 16 on everyday life.
		• Page 60 contains background information on everyday life.

3 A yard of a house.	The yard is an important part of the home; where animals are kept, or for sleeping, eating, washing and cooking.	• Use with activity sheets 15 and 16 on everyday and rural life. • Pages 60–64 contain information on everyday life and cooking.

4 Domestic activities:
  a Pumping water
  b Washing pans.
	These also illustrate activities taking place in a home's yard. The man at the pump illustrates the lack of running water in many homes. This man is comparatively lucky – many people (usually the women) have to walk to collect their water. The other photo shows a woman sitting on a typical bed, a charpoy made of woven string. Notice also the women washing outside.	• Use with activity sheets 6, 15, 16 and 18 on everyday life.
		• Pages 29 and 60 contain information on weather and everyday life.

5 Inside a home in Jodhpur:
  a Window
  b Kitchen.
	Notice the brightly-coloured material and decorated windows. A more modern kitchen is shown.	• Use with activity sheet 15 on everyday life.
		• Pages 59, 60 and 64 contain information on everyday life and cooking.

SCHOOLS 6 Going to school.	Education is free between the ages of 6 and 14, but many children in India still do not attend. There are public and private schools, with the emphasis of lessons in Rajasthan being on reading, writing, health skills and farming skills.	• Use with activity sheet 23 on school life. • Pages 56, 57 and 60 contain information on everyday and school life.

7 School assembly:
  a Front view of children praying
  b Side view.
	Notice that a great part of the school day will be in the open air, or semi-covered, and most of it also spent on the floor when desks and chairs cannot be afforded. Notice the painting of Nehru, independent India's first prime minister, on the hall wall.	• Use with activity sheet 23 on school life.
		• Pages 56 and 57 contain information on school life.

8 In the classroom.	Many schools still use slates for writing. The photograph shows a boy cleaning his.	• Use with activity sheet 23 on school life. • Pages 56 and 57 contain information on school life.
9 TulsiRam at school. 10 School lessons.	Children can use these to compare with their classroom environments and activities.	• Use with activity sheet 23 on school life. • Pages 56 and 57 contain information on school life.

Photo	Purpose	Links
WORK 11 Weaving wool.	Rajasthan produces 40% of India's wool. It is a rural primary industry – there are no wool processing plants yet.	• Use with activity sheet 10 on industry. • Page 34 contains background information on working life.
12 Dyed cloth drying.	The photograph shows cotton drying after being dyed. All towns and villages still colour and dye their own material. Dyes have traditionally been made from vegetables, plants, earth and insects.	• Use with activity sheets 10 and 14 on industry and tourism. • Pages 34 and 43 contain background information on industry and tourism.
13 Pottery.	A potter's shop – these exist in all Rajasthani towns and villages. Children can discuss their uses, materials and so on. They should also reflect on the impact factory-produced alternatives would have on the lives of potters.	• Posters 2 and 3. • Use with activity sheets 10, 18 and 24 on industry and tourism. • Pages 34 and 43 contain information on industry and tourism.
14 a Farming. b Harvest time.	In India, 62% of people work on the land, or depend on agriculture for a living. The figure is higher in Rajasthan. Most 'farms' are only tiny pieces of land, with families relying on this for food and income. The second photograph shows a woman at work cutting the crop in the dry fields.	• Poster 1. • Use with activity sheets 6, 15 and 16 on farming and climate. • Pages 28, 37, 44 and 46 contain information on farming.
15 Irrigation.	Here we see water being raised from an irrigation channel, essential for crops. Children need to compare these methods with farming methods in the UK.	• Poster 1. • Use with activity sheets 6, 15–17 on climate and farming. • Pages 24, 28, 44 and 46 contain information on climate and farming.
SHOPPING 16 Material shop.	Notice the bright colours – it is perhaps because the Rajasthani environment is so parched and brown that the people use such vivid colours.	• Use with activity sheets 10 and 19 on industry and shopping. • Pages 34 and 37 contain background information on industry.
17 Market stalls.	Markets sell anything – this photograph can be used to identify some of the things being sold. Notice also the clothes worn by the people in the photograph.	• Poster 4. • Use with activity sheet 16 on everyday life. • Page 51 contains information on shopping.
18 Street seller.	These illustrate typical stalls; one is a spice stall selling ready-made poppadoms. Spices are the most important ingredient in Indian cooking – sometimes 25 being used in one mixture. Children can find many of these in their own local supermarkets.	• Poster 4. • Use with activity sheet 15 on everyday life. • Pages 48, 51 and 64 contain information on shopping, farming and cooking.
19 a Grocer's shop. b Chemist's shop.	There are symbols which identify certain shops worldwide. Note that many Rajasthani shops have an open aspect, reflecting the climate. The upper photograph shows a typical lock-up store where goods are sold on the street but packed away in the evening.	• Poster 4. • Use with activity sheet 19 on shopping in Jodhpur. • Page 51 contains information on shopping.
20 Gift shop.	Income from tourism is becoming increasingly important in India. Puppet makers of Jodhpur are especially famous – puppetry being an ancient form of entertainment. The puppets are usually a metre in height, with wooden carved heads and two strings. Children can list other goods tourists might buy.	• Use with activity sheets 18 and 24 on puppets and tourism. • Pages 37, 50 and 60 contain background information on Jodhpur.

Poster 1
The Indian subcontinent

Images of the Indian subcontinent (poster with numbered photographs overlaid on a map of the Indian subcontinent)

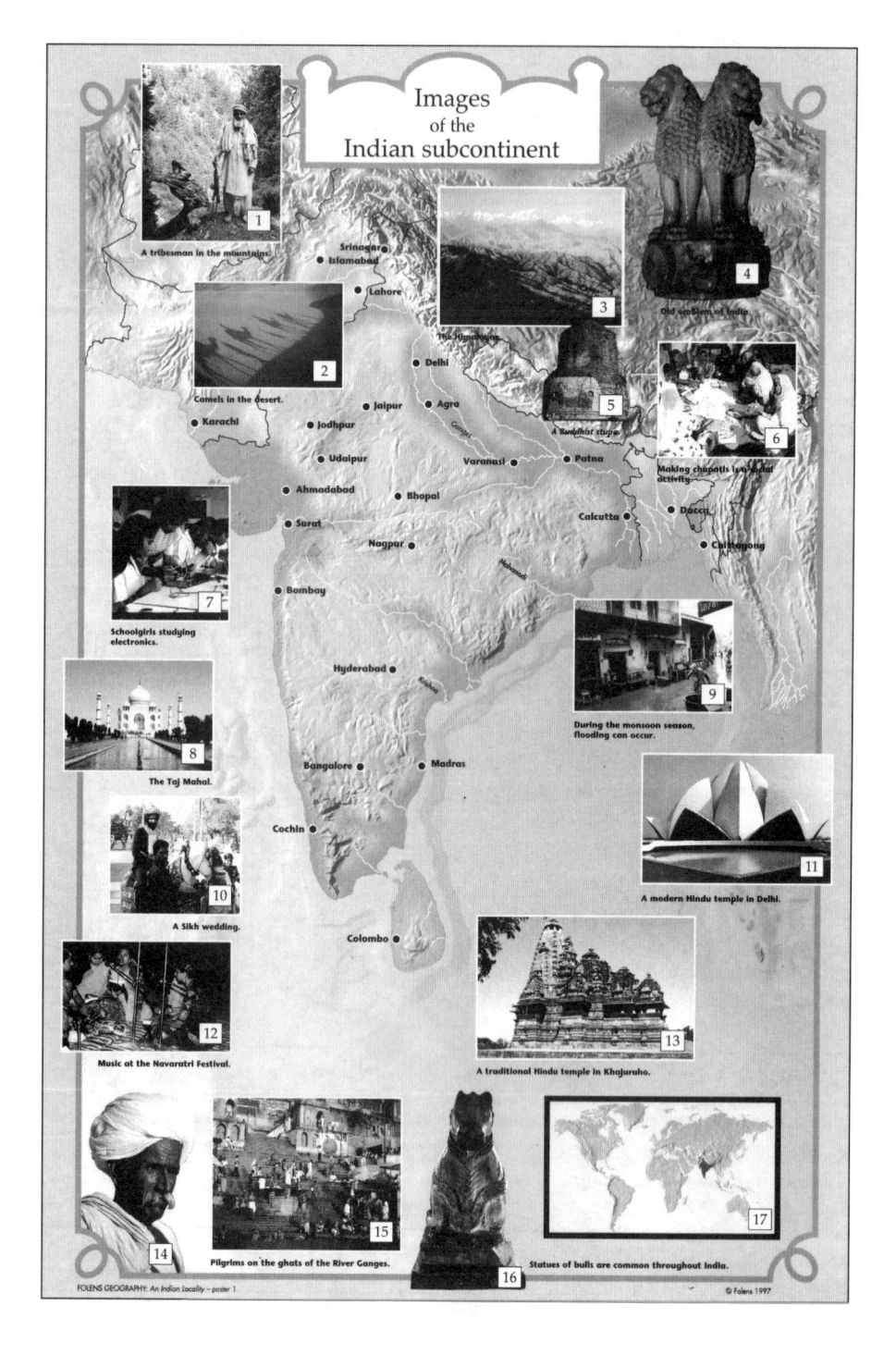

Labels on the map include: Srinagar, Islamabad, Lahore, Delhi, Jaipur, Agra, Karachi, Jodhpur, Udaipur, Varanasi, Patna, Ahmadabad, Bhopal, Surat, Nagpur, Calcutta, Dacca, Chittagong, Bombay, Hyderabad, Bangalore, Madras, Cochin, Colombo, The Himalayas.

Photo captions:
1. A tribesman in the mountains.
2. Camels in the desert.
3. (Mountain scene)
4. Old emblem of India.
5. A Buddhist stupa.
6. Making chapatis is a social activity.
7. Schoolgirls studying electronics.
8. The Taj Mahal.
9. During the monsoon season, flooding can occur.
10. A Sikh wedding.
11. A modern Hindu temple in Delhi.
12. Music at the Navaratri Festival.
13. A traditional Hindu temple in Khajuraho.
14. (Portrait)
15. Pilgrims on the ghats of the River Ganges.
16. Statues of bulls are common throughout India.
17. (World map)

FOLENS GEOGRAPHY: An Indian Locality – poster 1   © Folens 1997

Picture	Purpose	Links
1 Tribesman from frontier.	The mountains of north-west Pakistan are home to people who remain fiercely independent. Gun ownership is high.	• Use with activity sheet 15 on rural life. • Pages 24 and 44 contain information on farming.

8   FOLENS GEOGRAPHY: *An Indian Locality*   © Folens (not copiable)

Picture	Purpose	Links
2 Camels in desert.	Many children associate camels with North Africa but they are important in India and Pakistan.	• Use with activity sheets 16 and 17 on deserts. • Page 46 contains information on deserts.
3 Himalayan mountains.	The Himalayas contain the world's highest mountains. Formed by tectonic plate movements, they separate the subcontinent from Central Asia.	• Use with activity sheets 6 and 12 on climate. • Pages 24, 26–28 contain information on the region.
4 Traditional emblem of India.	King Ashoka of the Mauryan Dynasty ruled his empire on a theory based upon Buddhist principles. He inscribed his theory on stone columns on the top of which were four carved lions.	• Pages 16 and 24 contain background information on India.
5 Buddhist stupa.	Buddhism originated in India but is now a religion practised largely in south-east Asia. Buddhist buildings remain, however, as evidence of the past.	• Pages 24, 36 and 37 contain background information on India and religion.
6 Making chapatis.	Wheat and rice are the great 'staples' of diet in the subcontinent. Chapatis are a form of bread.	• Pages 44, 56, 60 and 64 contain information on cooking and everyday life.
7 Schoolgirls in an electronics class.	India has a growing range of technological industries. It is a major producer of software.	• Use with activity sheet 10 on industry. • Pages 24, 34, 37 and 50 contain information on everyday life.
8 Taj Mahal.	This was built in 1632 by Shah Jahan, in memory of his favourite wife Mumtaz Mahal. Its symmetry, location and craftsmanship make it one of the best-known buildings in the world.	• Use with activity sheet 14 on tourism. • Pages 40–41 contain information on tourism.
9 Flood.	The monsoon rains bring necessary water but also the threat of flooding. Environmental changes exacerbate the effects.	• Use with activity sheets 6 and 17 on climate. • Pages 26–27 contain information on the region.
10 An Indian wedding.	Most weddings in India are great affairs joining two people and their respective families. Feeding the guests can take all day. The photo shows a groom wearing a combination of modern and traditional clothing.	• Photo 17. • Use with activity sheet 16 on everyday life. • Page 36 contains information on religion.
11, 13 Hindu temples.	India is 90% Hindu. Temples range from ancient to modern. The two shown here are at Khajuraho (ancient) and Delhi (modern).	• Pages 24, 36 and 37 contain background information on India and religion.
12 Musicians.	Music features strongly at Hindu festivals, with women playing a prominent part. The photo is of the Navaratri Festival (Festival of the Nine Nights).	• Pages 36 and 37 contain information on everyday life.
14 Man with turban.	Turbans provide insulation from the desert heat. They are worn by many in the Indian subcontinent, not just Sikhs.	• Use with activity sheet 16. • Pages 36 and 46 contain information on religion and desert life.
15 Ganges.	A major source of economy but also a holy river, the Ganges is a site of pilgrimage to Hindus, who bathe in the water. The dead have their ashes scattered on it.	• Use with activity sheet 6 on climate and weather. • Pages 26 and 27 contain information on the region.
16 Bull.	The bull motif is found in the Indus Valley civilisation and continues to the present day. This one is at Khajuraho.	• Activity sheets 1–4 and pages 18 and 19 contain information on the Indus Valley.
17 World map.	Showing the position and size of the Indian subcontinent in relation to the rest of the world.	• Pages 26 and 27 contain maps of India.

© Folens (not copiable) FOLENS GEOGRAPHY: *An Indian Locality*

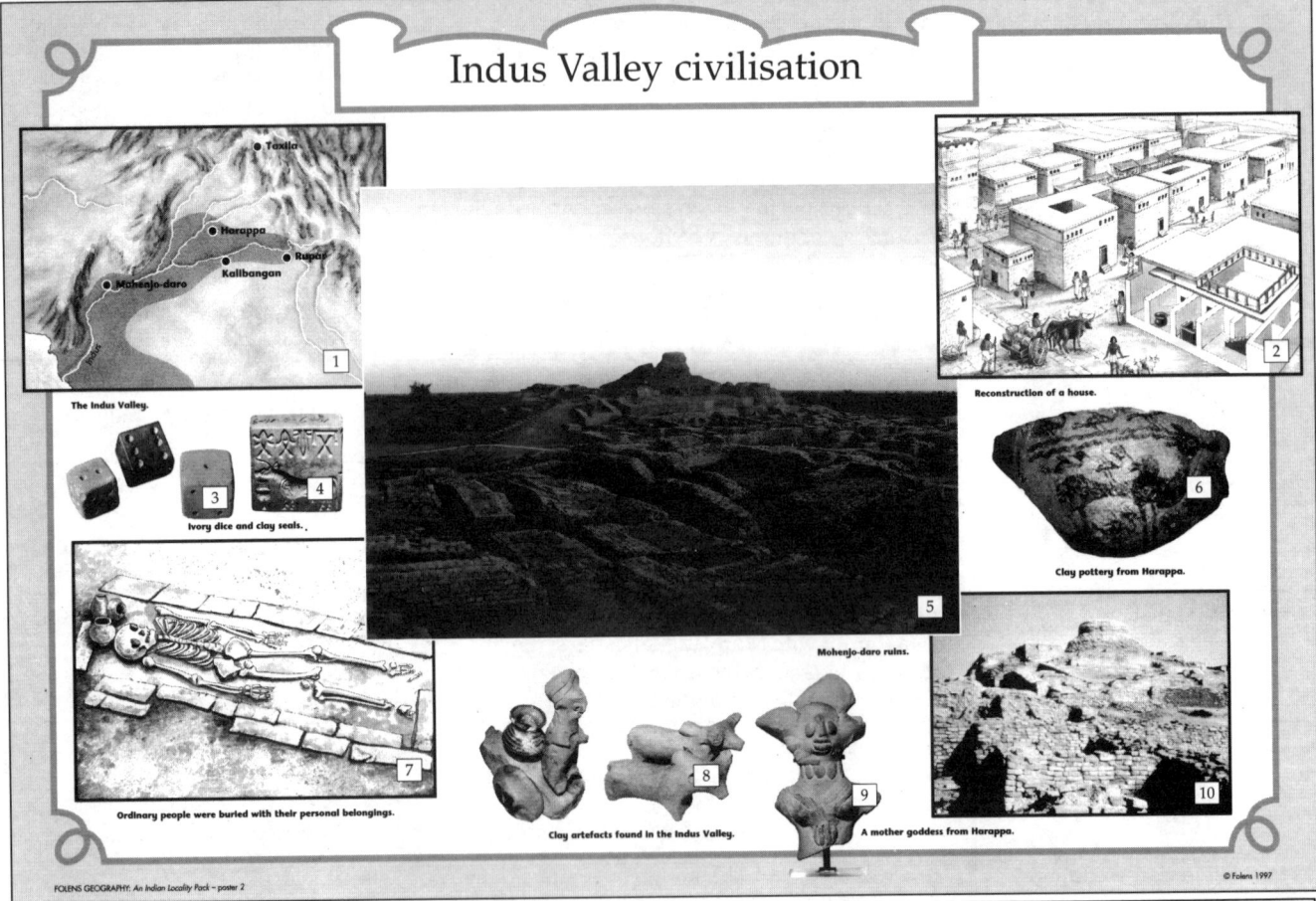

Poster 2
Indus Valley civilisation

Indus Valley civilisation

The Indus Valley. (1)
Reconstruction of a house. (2)
Ivory dice and clay seals. (3, 4)
Mohenjo-daro ruins. (5)
Clay pottery from Harappa. (6)
Ordinary people were buried with their personal belongings. (7)
Clay artefacts found in the Indus Valley. (8)
A mother goddess from Harappa. (9)
(10)

Picture		Purpose	Links
1	A map of the Indus Valley.	The map illustrates the location and extent of settlement in the Indus Valley.	• Use with activity sheets 16, 18 and 19.
2	Reconstruction of a house.	To show the style, size and materials used.	• Use with activity sheets 1 and 2 on the Indus Valley.
3	Dice.	These artefacts interestingly have the same patterns as modern dice. They illustrate that the people must have had time to play games.	• Use with activity sheet 1. • Pages 18 and 19 contain information on the Indus Valley.
4	Seals and writing.	The seals illustrate the type of writing found. It has not yet been deciphered.	• Use with activity sheets 1 and 3 on the Indus Valley.
5 and 10	Mohenjo-daro ruins.	These photographs show the ruins of one of the most important cities of the Indus Valley civilisation.	• Use with activity sheets 1 and 2 on the Indus Valley.
6	Clay pottery.	An example of pottery found – some of which recorded stories in picture form.	• Use with activity sheet 1 on the Indus Valley.
7	Grave and skeleton.	Graves such as this show examples of personal belongings of the Indus people.	• Use with activity sheets 1 and 2 on the Indus Valley.
8	Bullocks and cart.	This artefact illustrates that farming was important in ancient times, as in Rajasthan today, and that the people had knowledge of the wheel.	• Photos 14 and 15. • Use with activity sheet 1 on the Indus Valley.
9	Stone figure found in Harappa.	This is thought to be the Earth Goddess and shows the importance of goddesses to Indus Valley life.	• Use with activity sheet 1 on the Indus Valley.

Poster 3
Everyday life in Rajasthan

[Poster image: Everyday life in Rajasthan, with numbered photographs 1–18 including captions: "Land of contrasts" (1), "Making pots is a skilled job" (5), "Women and men work together in the towns and countryside", "Time to relax" (12), "Women wash clothes in rivers, lakes and reservoirs", "Many people work in tourism" (15).]

Picture	Purpose	Links
1 Mother and child.	Bright tie-dyed saris and veils provide the characteristic dress of Rajasthani women. Different towns dye their material with their own distinctive methods and colours. The colour, design and cut can give indications of the village and caste of the wearer, the jewellery displaying their wealth.	• Pages 47 and 59 contain background information on everyday life.
2 The Thar Desert.	The Thar Desert covers more than half of the total area of Rajasthan. It has not always been so large and dry throughout history – the north-western edges supported the Indus civilisation and it is possible that human misuse of the land has actually helped to create more desert.	• Use with activity sheet 4 on the Indus Valley. • Pages 18, 19, 26, 27 and 39 contain information on the Indus Valley and Rajasthan.
3 and 9 Building site and mixing cement.	Notice the age of the children working in these photographs – many children still do not receive regular schooling and village families will depend on their income. Notice too the tank of water.	• Use with activity sheet 23 on school life. • Pages 37, 50, 56–57 and 60 contain information on school and everyday life.

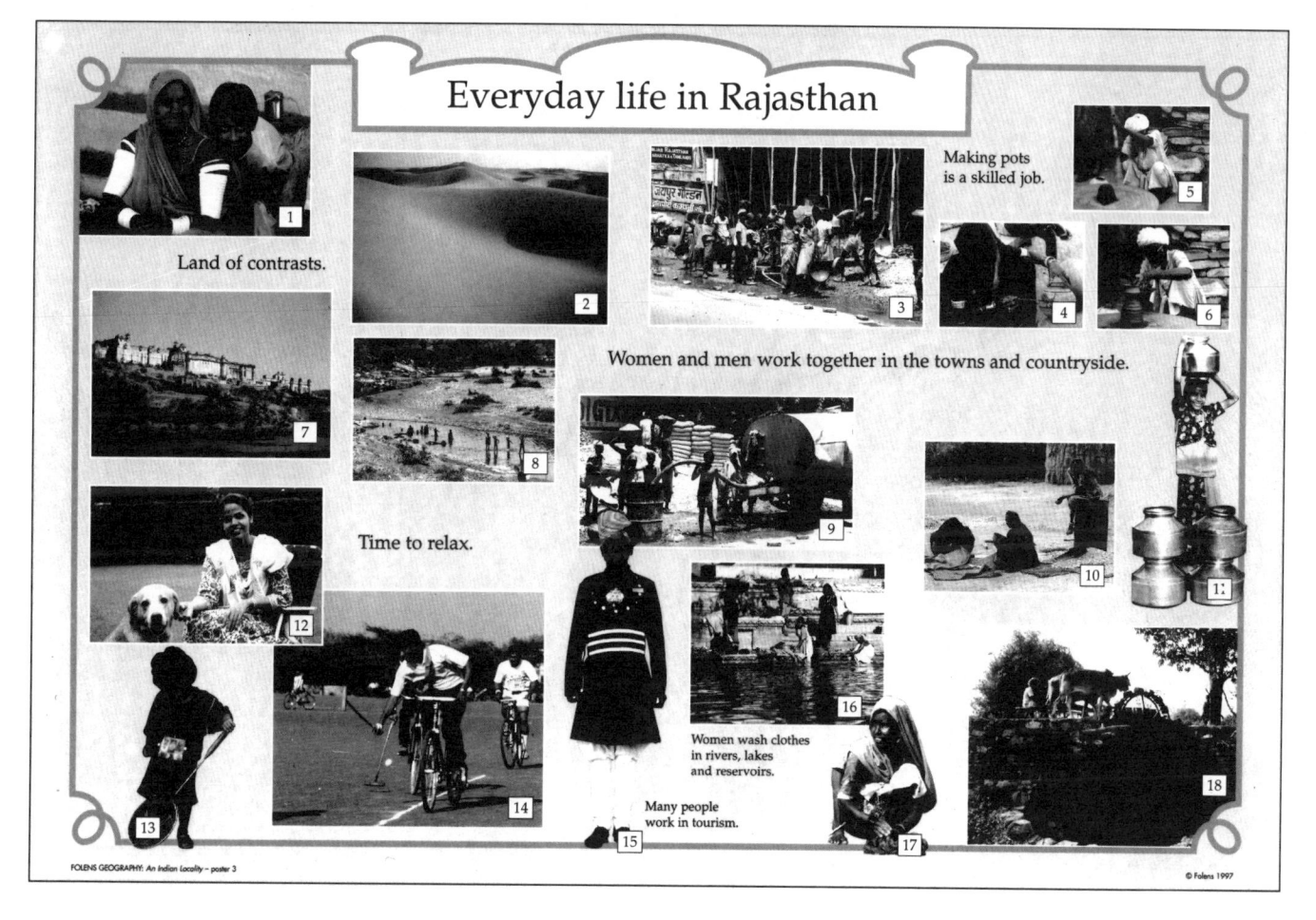

© Folens (not copiable)   FOLENS GEOGRAPHY: An Indian Locality   11

Picture	Purpose	Links
4–6 A potter.	In Rajasthan, perhaps more than any area of India, traditional crafts have been continued. In many towns and villages craftsmen have continued to hand down their skills through generations. Here you see pots being made and decorated. They are usually made from red terracotta.	• Use with activity sheet 10 on trade and industry. • Pages 34 and 60 contain information on industry and everyday life.
7 Jaisalmer Fort.	Jaisalmer provides another example of the impressive fortified towns typical of Rajasthan. It is often called 'The Jewel of the Desert', rising up from the middle of the Thar Desert. It is one of the oldest Rajasthani forts, built in the twelfth century.	• Use with activity sheets 13, 14, 16 and 18 on tourism and everyday life. • Pages 36–37 and 41 contain information on religion and tourism.
8, 11, 16 and 17 Water – a scarce commodity.	These images illustrate the standard of living of many people in Rajasthan. Very few homes have water or access to sanitation. Water is used from rivers and wells for all aspects of daily life. For women especially, the collection of water is a daily task.	• Use with activity sheets 5–6, 7–8 and 17 on weather, travel and population. • Pages 24, 28, 37 and 46 contain information on climate and deserts.
10 Women winnowing.	Women in their characteristic dress have been winnowing grain (bajra).	• Poster 1. • Photos 14 and 15. Use with activity sheets 15 and 16 on farming and everyday life. • Page 44 contains information on farming.
12 Woman and dog.	Middle class Indians live comfortable lives. In the past 20 years the middle classes have grown considerably.	• Pages 50, 56–57 and 60 contain information on school and everyday life.
13 A child playing in the street.	The climate allows children to play outside from an early age.	• Use with activity sheets 6 and 9 on climate and street life.
14 Tennis and cycle polo.	Polo, pigsticking and tennis were favourite sports of the Rajasthani royals. Jodhpur has produced some of the most outstanding polo players. Polo is still popular, particularly on bicycles.	• Use with activity sheets 20–21 on Jodhpur. • Page 50 contains information on tourism.
15 A doorman of a palace hotel.	Many of the wonderful Indian palaces are now being used as hotels for tourists. Doormen are proud to wear the traditional dress of Rajasthan.	• Use with activity sheets 4–5, 13–14 and 18 on tourism. • Page 41 contains information on tourism.
18 Irrigation.	This photograph shows that traditional methods of irrigation – a bullock turning a water wheel – are still very common today. It illustrates the problem of lack of water faced by farmers working on the desert soil. Less than 20% of cultivated land is irrigated and in recent years there have been severe droughts.	• Poster 1. • Photos 14 and 15. • Use with activity sheets 6, 15–17 on climate and everyday life. • Pages 28 and 46 contain information on climate and deserts.

FOLENS GEOGRAPHY: An Indian Locality

© Folens (not copiable)

Poster 4
Everyday life in Jodhpur

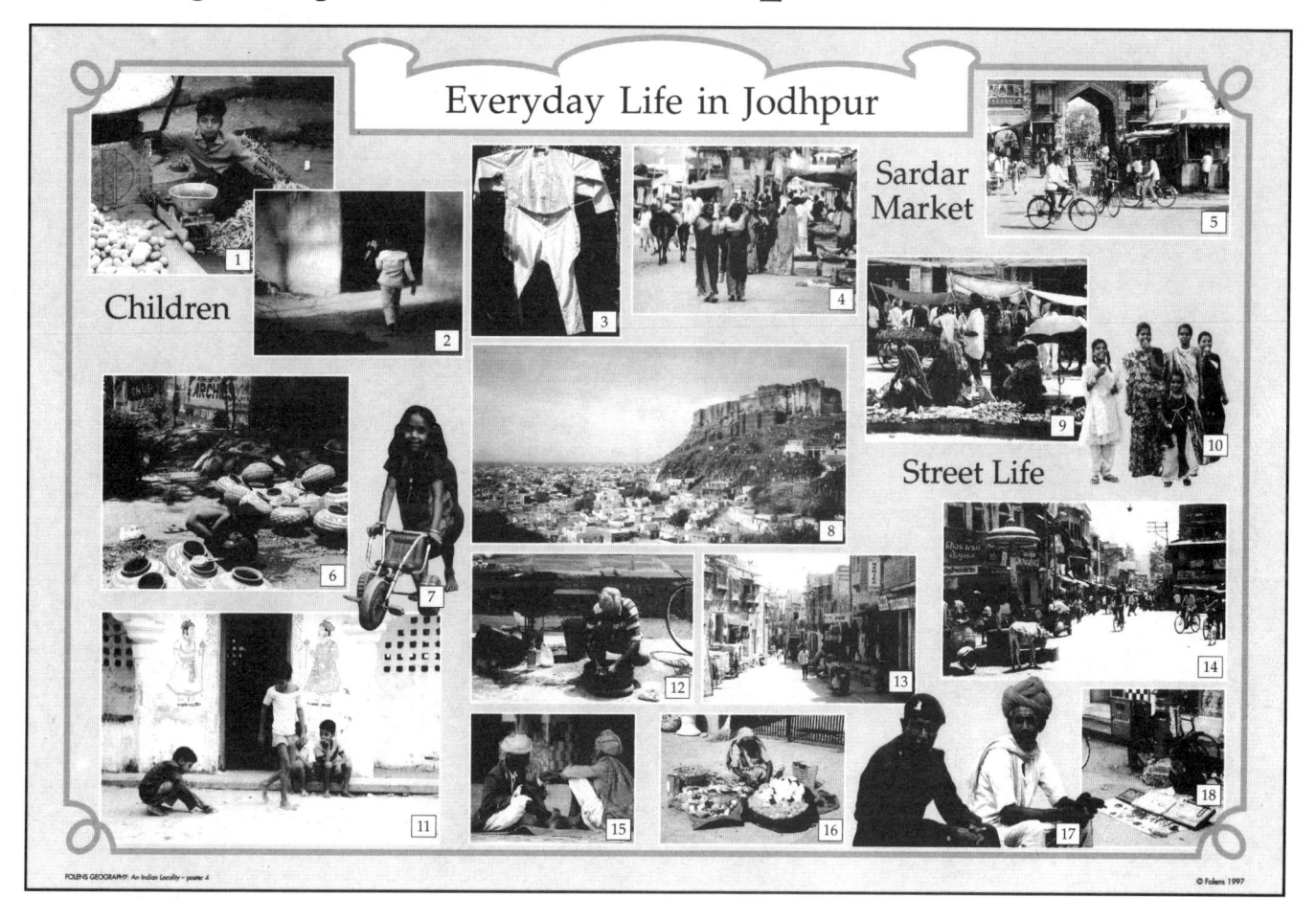

Picture	Purpose	Links
1, 2, 6, 7 and 11 Children of Jodhpur.	Examples of children at play. Children can compare these images with their own lifestyles.	• Photos 6–10. • Activity sheets 6, 19 and 23. • Pages 56 and 60.
3 Jodhpurs.	The trousers that take their name from Jodhpur.	• Page 50.
9, 12, 18 Street sellers.	Jodhpur's back streets are full of traditional craftsmen selling their wares.	• Photos 16–18. • Activity sheets 10 and 16. • Pages 19 and 34.
5 Sardar Bazaar Market.	This illustrates a busy section of Jodhpur, inside the old city walls. Notice the number of bicycles.	• Photos 17–18. • Activity sheets 19–21. Page 52.
8 General view of Jodhpur.	This photograph shows Meherangarh Fort and the blue-painted buildings of the city.	• Activity sheets 20, 22 on Jodhpur. • Pages 50 and 52.
4, 10 Indian women.	Notice the traditional saris.	• Poster 3, photos 1 and 5. • Activity sheet 19.
13 and 14 Shops.	These show other shopping streets in Jodhpur, which can be compared to streets in the children's own locality.	• Use with activity sheet 19. • Pages 36 and 51.
15 and 17 Local men.	The different styles and colours of turbans denote class, caste and religion of the wearer.	• Use with activity sheet 16. • Pages 36 and 46.
16 Flower seller.	Another street seller – flowers being sold at the entrance to a temple for placing on the shrine.	• Use with activity sheet 19. • Pages 36 and 51.

© Folens (not copiable) FOLENS GEOGRAPHY: An Indian Locality

Poster 5
Transport

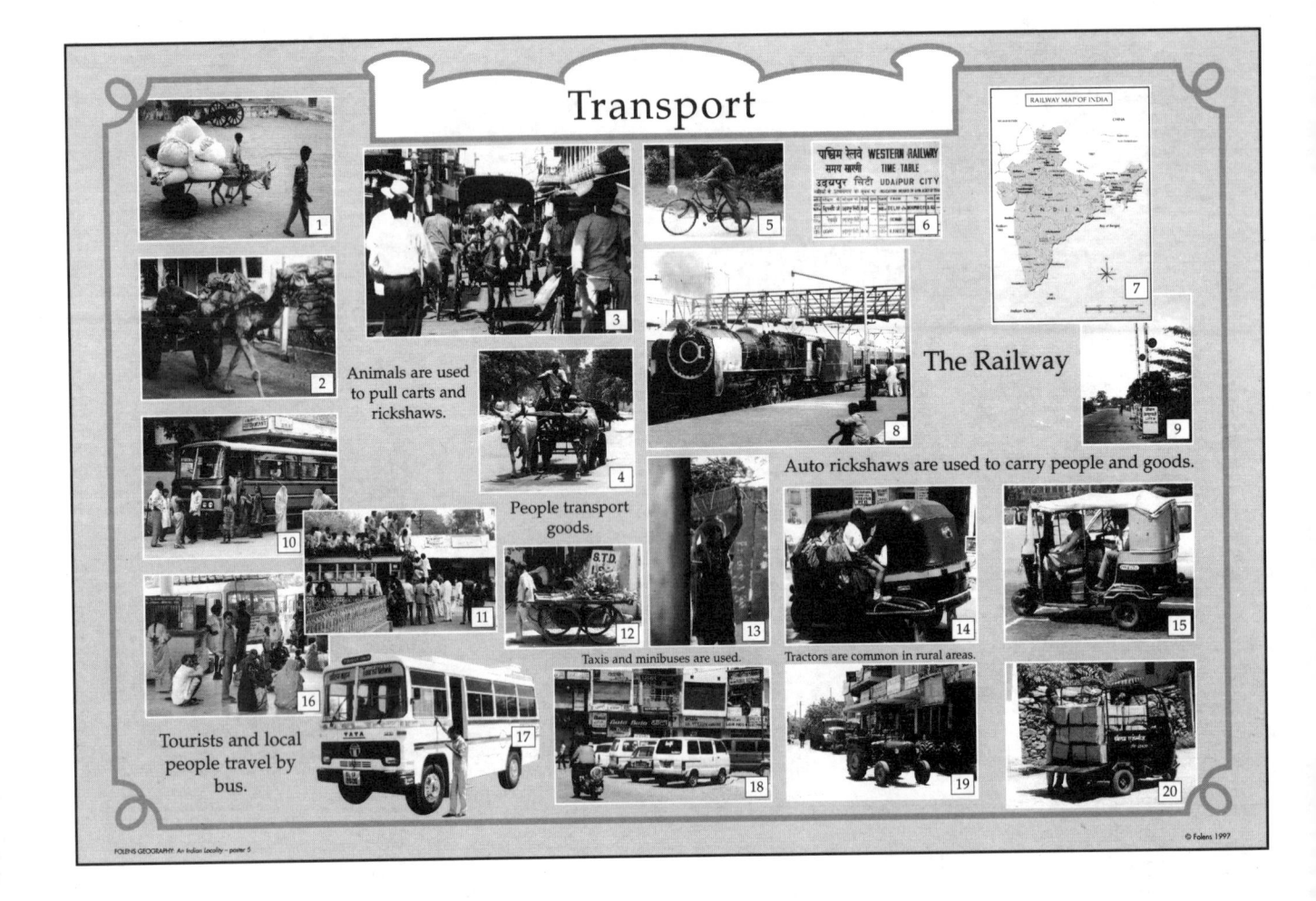

Transport

Poster image with 20 numbered photographs showing various forms of transport:
- Animals are used to pull carts and rickshaws.
- People transport goods.
- The Railway
- Auto rickshaws are used to carry people and goods.
- Taxis and minibuses are used.
- Tractors are common in rural areas.
- Tourists and local people travel by bus.

Picture	Purpose	Links
1 Donkey pulling a cart.	An important animal for work – carrying goods and people. Children can compare this image with methods of transport for work in their own locality.	• Use with activity sheets 10 and 15 on trade and rural life. • Pages 34 and 44 on farming and working life.
2 Camel and cart.	Camels are a very important part of everyday life in Rajasthan. They can be seen everywhere, especially in desert regions, for carrying people, transporting goods, pulling carts and so on. Camels are still the most common form of transport in the desert.	• Use with activity sheets 15 and 16 on desert and everyday life. • Pages 44 and 46 contain information on deserts and farming.
3, 14, 15 and 20 Auto rickshaws.	These crowd the streets of towns and cities. They are open, small and nippy. People can easily enter and leave and they take up little road space.	• Use with activity sheets 19 and 20 on Jodhpur. Page 52 contains information on Jodhpur.

FOLENS GEOGRAPHY: *An Indian Locality*

Picture	Purpose	Links
4 Bullocks and cart.	Cattle are found throughout India – for work and for their milk, meat and leather. Many farms still use traditional bullock ploughs.	• Photos 14–15. • Use with activity sheet 15 on everyday life. • Pages 34 and 44 contain information on farming life.
5 Man on bicycle.	The bicycle is the most common form of transport after walking. The bicycle industry is one of the largest industries in India.	• Use with activity sheets 9, 13 and 14 on travel and tourism. • Pages 32, 40 and 41 contain information on travel and tourism.
6–9 Trains and railways.	A popular form of travelling. There are over 61 000km of track. Notice the different classes of train. Steam trains still operate in Rajasthan. The guard in the picture is the guard of the Maharajah of Jodhpur's train, used by tourists.	• Use with activity sheets 9 and 20 on travel and tourism. • Page 32 contains information on train travel.
10, 11, 16 and 17 Coaches.	There are good coach links between major towns and cities. Local buses are often overcrowded. The tourist coach is built by Tata – a major name in Indian industry. Tata vehicles are now exported widely.	• Photos 16–19. • Use with activity sheets 9 and 20 on travel and tourism.
12 Hand-pulled cart.	Another example of the variety of transport used for work. Many street markets are served by traders who bring their produce into town in the early morning using carts such as this.	• Photos 14–15. • Use with activity sheet 15 on everyday life. • Pages 34 and 44 contain information on farming life.
13 Indian woman carrying wood.	Wood is used as a fuel, for heating and cooking. As trees are cut down women have to travel further to collect fuel. Note the bright clothing despite the practical side to the task.	• Pages 47 and 59 contain background information on everyday life.
18 A taxi rank.	Minibuses run regular services to local villages from most towns.	• Use with activity sheets 9 and 20 on travel and tourism.
19 Tractor.	Many children imagine **all** Indian farmers work small plots for subsistence. In fact farmers with larger farms have their own tractors and others can easily hire them as necessary through the year.	• Photos 14–15. • Use with activity sheet 15 on everyday life. • Pages 34 and 44 contain information on farming life.

India time line

c 35 000BC
The earliest known civilisation of South Asia emerged in the Indus Valley, corresponding to the Bronze Age cultures of Ancient Egypt, Mesopotamia and Crete. The remains of settlements have been found throughout the Indus River Valley in modern Pakistan, west along the coast to the Iranian border and in India's north-western states such as Rajasthan. This was one of the largest geographical areas populated by a Bronze Age culture.

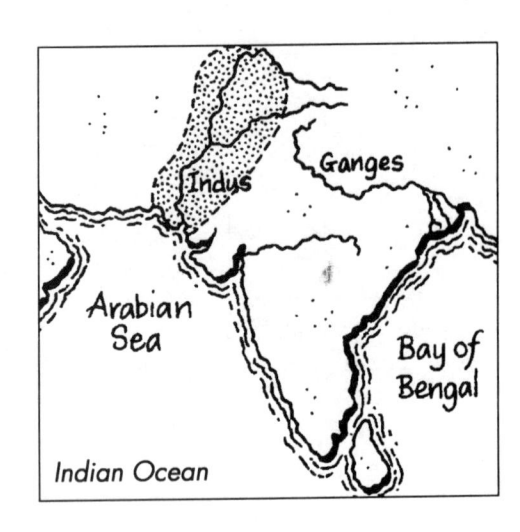

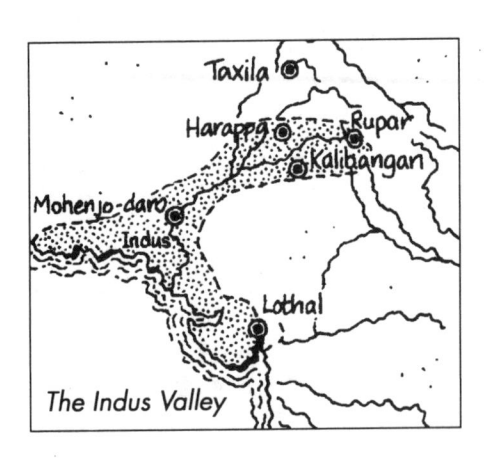

2500–1500BC
The Harappa culture of city dwellers, traders and builders grew out of the early Indus Valley culture. Excavated settlements show mud-brick buildings separated by streets, and the cities, such as Mohenjo-daro and Harappa, had large public buildings. These buildings were thought to be colleges, granaries and palaces.

The Indus Valley civilisation covered part of modern Rajasthan.

1500–1000BC
Aryan tribes from the Caucasus region to the north invaded India and settled mainly in the Punjab region. They brought the chariot with them and their arrival began a series of wars. The Vedic religion which they brought with them was the forerunner of Hinduism and the caste system.

600–500BC
Buddhism was founded by Prince Siddartha Gautama (the Buddha) and Jainism by Vardamana Jnatputra (Mahavira). Both religions began in northern India.

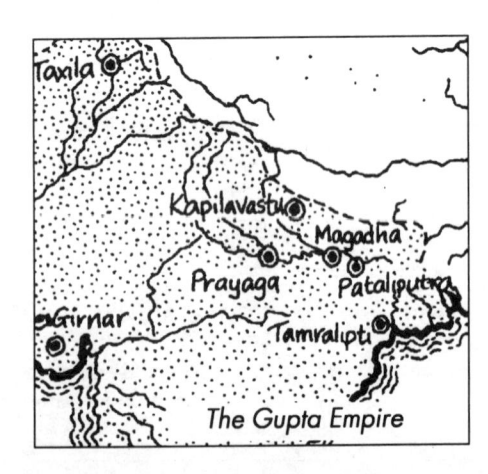

326BC
Alexander the Great led an expedition into northern India and took control of a large area of north-western and central India. Although this did not affect India's history greatly, the art, sculpture and science of the Greeks did have an effect in northern India.

321–185BC
The Mauryan Dynasty. Ashoka became India's first emperor.

AD320–535
The Gupta Empire. Trade with the Middle East and Roman Empire made India richer. This was a golden age of arts and sciences.

AD520
The Huns invaded and began the end of the Gupta Empire.

FOLENS GEOGRAPHY: *An Indian Locality*

8th to 11th centuries AD
Arab invasions brought Islam to northern India. The Rajputs began to appear in north-west India, building up their own power, but often fighting each other.

1398
The first Mongol invasion led by Timur (an heir of Genghis Khan).

1498
Vasco da Gama discovered the sea route from Europe to the East and European interest in India grew.

1526
The second Mughal invasion. There were 17 Mughal (from the word Mongol) emperors who created the golden age of Indian culture. Forts at Delhi, Agra and in Rajasthan as well as the Taj Mahal were built at this time.

1618
The British East India Company was allowed to trade and British influence began to spread over India. The Mughal Empire began to crumble.

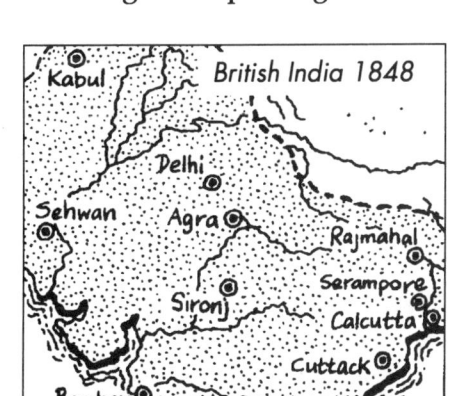

1757
Robert Clive won control of Bengal at the Battle of Plassey.

1799
The Duke of Wellington conquered a large part of southern India.

1857–1858
The Indian Mutiny, or first war of Indian independence, was crushed and Britain took full control of India, which became part of the British Empire.

1877
Queen Victoria became Empress of India.

1914–1918
Many Indians fought on Britain's side in the First World War.

1920
National movement led by Mohandas 'Mahatma' Gandhi (Mahatma – means 'Great Soul') to gain independence peacefully.

1939–1945
Indians again serve Britain in a world war.

1947
British India was divided into India and Pakistan. Jawaharlal Nehru became India's first prime minister. Twelve million Muslims, Sikhs and Hindus moved their homes because of the split. Gandhi was assassinated in 1948.

1949
The Maharajahs joined the Indian union. Their 23 states became Rajasthan ('Land of the Rajahs').

1974
India exploded its first atomic bomb.

1984
Prime Minister Indira Gandhi was assassinated.

1990
Conflict over the Kashmir region between India and Pakistan. Rajiv Gandhi was assassinated by Tamil extremists in 1991.

1997
India's population exceeds 900 000 000, second only to China.

The Indus Valley civilisation

Activities

The Indian subcontinent is the home of the Indus Valley civilisation. It started 4500 years ago along the valley of the Indus River, and covered an area of more than a million square miles – land which is now in India and Pakistan. Sites have been discovered in Mohenjo-daro, Harappa and Chanhu-daro in Pakistan and Lothal and Kalibangan in India. Almost all our knowledge comes from the work of archaeologists. The people of Rajasthan have their origins in one of the world's oldest civilisations.

Here are some suggested activities to accompany the following children's pages:

- Average rainfall in modern-day Rajasthan is lower than rainfall at the time of the Indus civilisation, which is one reason why there is not the same amount of sustainable agriculture in the region. Discuss with the children reasons why life has changed in the area – such as desertification through overgrazing, clearance of woodland in ancient times and so on.

- The decline in rainfall, earthquakes (it lies in an earthquake zone), changes in the course of the river and epidemic diseases are other suggestions for the end of the civilisation, which can be discussed with the children.

- Compare the area of the Indus Valley with a map of India, and Rajasthan. Children can mark on modern cities and compare these locations with the ancient sites.

- Compare the types of homes, building materials, sewage systems and so on with modern-day villages and towns in Rajasthan. In what ways are they similar or different?

- The great bath was an important discovery.

- The children can research its discovery – what it was like and what it might have been used for.

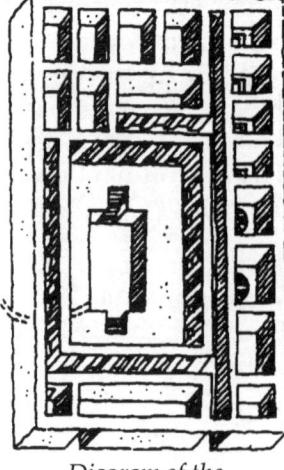

Diagram of the public bath of Mohenjo-daro.

- Lothal was an important port on the coast – the centre for trade with other countries – and seals from Lothal have been found in Mesopotamia. The children can look at a map of the ancient world and look at places where the Indus people might have sailed, plotting routes for the sailing ships.

- Cemeteries have been excavated. Children might research burial customs and beliefs of the Indus people, which can be compared with other civilisations. No large temples were found in the Indus Valley; instead there were hundreds of small shrines.

- The children can design their own Indus pottery. They can choose a well-known legend – especially stories which involve animals (eg Aesop's fables) – to tell through illustration. The children can compare Indus Valley pottery with that of the Ancient Greeks – are there any similarities?

- The children can compare what we know of the religious beliefs and practices with those of Ancient Egypt and Greece. What effect does the lack of written records have? The children can examine examples of Indus writing. Can they suggest any interpretations?

- Give the children a set of objects which you have collected (such as teddy bear, umbrella, clog and so on). The objects are to have belonged to an imaginary person. The children use the 'artefacts' to work as archaeologists and build a picture of the person who used them.

pupil information sheet 1

The Indus Valley civilisation

3000BC   AD500

Ancient Greece
Ancient Egypt
Indus Valley

The Indus river is one of the great rivers of Asia, flowing from the Himalayas to the sea through Pakistan.

In the 1920s, two large mounds were found in the river valley. These were excavated by archaeologists and the remains of large cities were found. They were thousands of years old.

The people who lived in these cities were the people of the Indus Valley civilisation. There were about a hundred towns and villages and five large cities in the area. Archaeologists discovered that the people were mainly farmers but that they also traded with other countries. They traded their crafts and farm produce for precious metals and cloth.

The Indus Valley people did not have many raw materials so they had to trade with other countries.

Traders had a system of weights and measures, made from polished stone.

The two most important cities found were at Mohenjo-daro and Harappa. These cities were well planned and even had their own underground drains. They were planned on a grid system with straight streets.

Houses were made of bricks which had been baked hard in a kiln. Each house had its own bathroom, well and drain connected to the main drains. They were usually laid out round a yard. Stairs have been discovered so they had two or three floors.

Small houses have been found on the corners of streets which might have been for night watchmen or police.

This is what a house might have looked like:

A drain running down the street.
The little picture shows what a toilet looked like.

© Folens (copiable page)   FOLENS GEOGRAPHY: An Indian Locality

activity sheet 1

Indus Valley artefacts

Here are examples of evidence which has been found. They tell us about the lives of the people who lived in the Indus Valley.

You need
- poster 2

- Clay models like these bullocks and cart have been found in Harappa. This shows that the Indus people knew about wheels but no wheels have been excavated.

- Some pots were found at Lothal. They were decorated with paintings of animals. The pictures may have told stories.

- Lots of sculptures and jewellery have been found. Here is a baked clay sculpture of a goddess.

- People of the Indus Valley used picture writing, but no one has been able to translate what it says. This writing is on seals which people might have used as signatures on clay documents. They have pictures of animals, such as rhinos and elephants. Pictures of boats have also been found on seals.

- This is a statue of a priest king which was found in a small house in Mohenjo-daro.

- These dice are made of limestone. Notice that the patterns for the numbers are the same as a modern dice.

1. What does this evidence tell us about life of the ancient Indus Valley civilisation?
2. Copy and complete this chart to record your ideas.

artefact	what was it made from?	what was it used for?	what does it tell us about the life of the people?

FOLENS GEOGRAPHY: An Indian Locality © Folens (copiable page)

activity sheet 2

A city in the Indus Valley

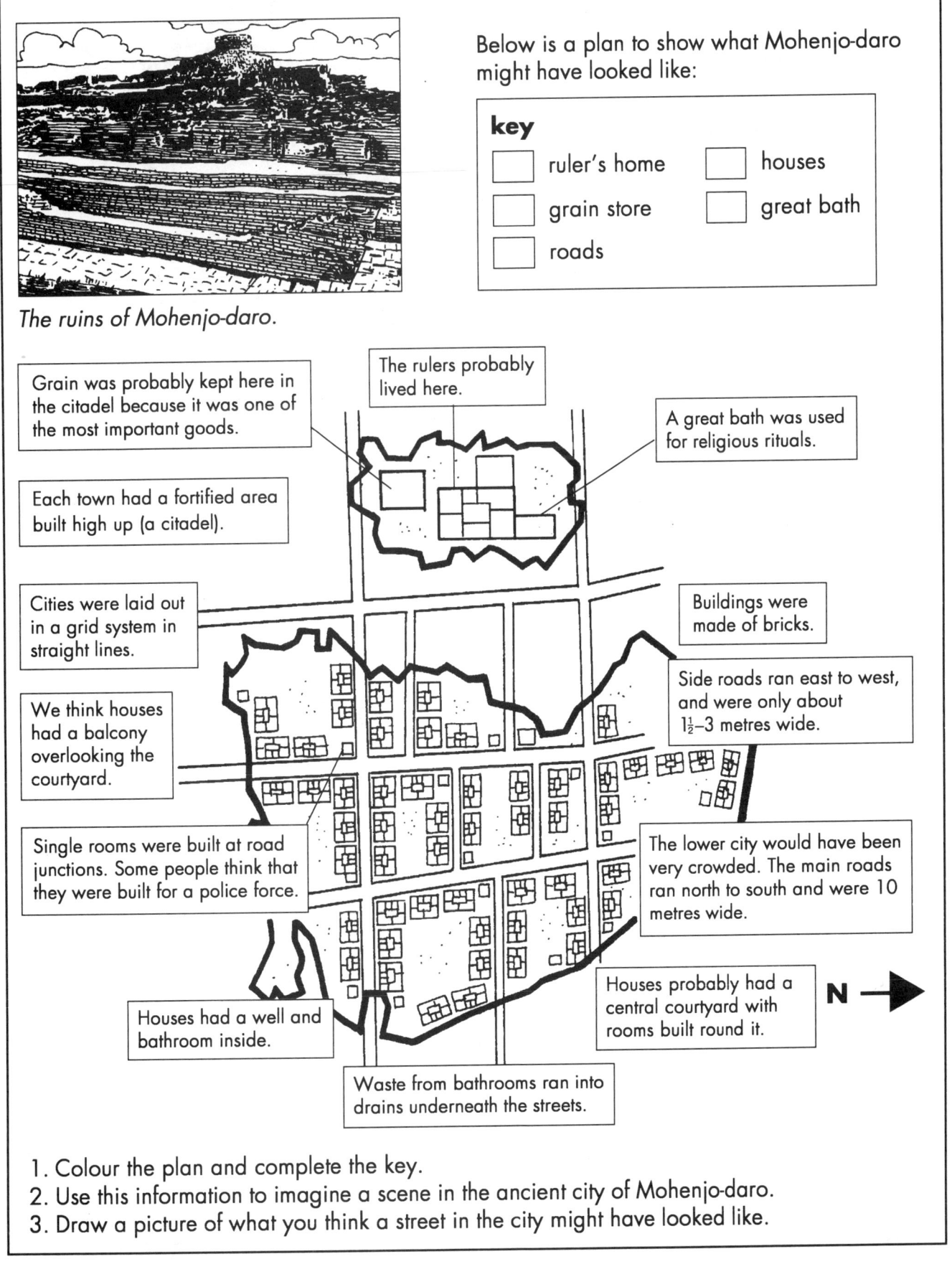

The ruins of Mohenjo-daro.

Below is a plan to show what Mohenjo-daro might have looked like:

key
- ☐ ruler's home
- ☐ houses
- ☐ grain store
- ☐ great bath
- ☐ roads

Grain was probably kept here in the citadel because it was one of the most important goods.

The rulers probably lived here.

A great bath was used for religious rituals.

Each town had a fortified area built high up (a citadel).

Cities were laid out in a grid system in straight lines.

Buildings were made of bricks.

Side roads ran east to west, and were only about 1½–3 metres wide.

We think houses had a balcony overlooking the courtyard.

Single rooms were built at road junctions. Some people think that they were built for a police force.

The lower city would have been very crowded. The main roads ran north to south and were 10 metres wide.

Houses had a well and bathroom inside.

Houses probably had a central courtyard with rooms built round it.

Waste from bathrooms ran into drains underneath the streets.

N →

1. Colour the plan and complete the key.
2. Use this information to imagine a scene in the ancient city of Mohenjo-daro.
3. Draw a picture of what you think a street in the city might have looked like.

© Folens (copiable page) FOLENS GEOGRAPHY: *An Indian Locality* 21

activity sheet 3

Make your own Indus Valley seal

Over 2000 small seals, made of soapstone, have been discovered in the Indus Valley. It is thought that they were used as personal stamps, like a signature.

1. Design your own personal seal.

2. Which animal do you think would represent your character?

   Try to copy some of the Indus writing.

3. Now make your seal out of clay. Think about how you will carve the clay so that it will leave a print.

4. Use paints to make the print.

FOLENS GEOGRAPHY: *An Indian Locality* © Folens (copiable page)

activity sheet 4

What happened to the people of the Indus Valley?

The Indus Valley civilisation was well organised, and was one of the largest of the ancient world, but it did not last as long as other ancient civilisations such as Egypt or Greece. Historians and archaeologists have tried to explain why and what might have happened to the people.

Clue 1   Bricks fired in a kiln
The buildings were made from fire-hardened bricks. Trees had to be cut down for fuel for the kilns. Lots of wood would be needed.

Clue 2   Skeletons
Skeletons have been found with deep marks in their skulls. The houses had been burned.

Clue 3   The Rig Veda
The *Rig Veda* is a collection of ancient stories. They talk about people (Aryans) who moved into northern India with sheep and cattle, looking for grazing land. They were great warriors and rode on horses. They knew how to make weapons of iron.

Historians and archaeologists have also used their imaginations to suggest what might have happened.

Suggestion 1   An ancient Indian story
"A man named Manu befriended a fish just before the great flood which engulfed the earth. The grateful fish warned Manu about the coming disaster and advised him to build a ship for his own safety. When the flood came, the fish was able to tow Manu and the ship to the only mountain peak which stood above the flood water. Alone, of all the world's people, Manu was saved. He became the source from which all mankind sprang. He drew up a code of laws by which all the people of the earth were to live."

Suggestion 2   Crops and animals
We know the Indus people grew their own crops and kept animals. As the population grew, more crops and animals would be needed.

Suggestion 3   Water
Too much salt in water can make the soil poor. When the Indus flooded it is possible that the land became polluted with salt.

- Look at each of these possible causes for the end of the Indus civilisation. What does each one mean? What would the consequences be for the people of the Indus Valley? Set out your answers in a chart like this:

Cause	Consequence
Fired Bricks	All the trees were chopped down and there was no wood left for building or for fuel. Animals that were hunted left the area. Floods washed the soil away in the monsoons.
Skeletons	
'Rig Veda'	
Ancient story	

© Folens (copiable page)   FOLENS GEOGRAPHY: *An Indian Locality*

A snapshot of India

India is the seventh largest country in the world, its area being approximately 3 330 000 km^2, thirteen times the size of the UK. Six countries border India: Pakistan, China, Nepal, Bhutan, Bangladesh and Myanmar (formerly Burma).

Pakistan and Bangladesh used to be part of India until the country was divided in 1947, when India became independent after ninety years of British rule. No one knows how many people lost their lives in the two years of violence which followed, but 12–14 million people were made homeless, half fleeing from Pakistan to India, the rest making the journey the other way. India became a republic and is the world's largest democracy, made up of 26 states and seven union territories (islands and large cities). The President is the head of state, and the Prime Minister the head of government. Most people think of India as one country, but it is in fact a collection of cultures, religions and different ways of life spread across a vast area.

The population

The population of India is around 903 million people – approximately 17% of all the people in the world, second only to the population of China. The largest cities are Calcutta with 10 million inhabitants, Bombay 9 million, Delhi 5.7 million and Madras 5 million. The capital is New Delhi. About 80% of Indian people live in villages.

Landscape

India has a very varied landscape, snow-capped mountains, tropical rainforest, deserts and beaches. It can, however, be split easily into four main geographical regions:
1. The mountains which mark India's northern boundary – the Himalayas.
2. Where the River Ganges flows from the Himalayas, across the flat plain – called the Indo-Gangetic Plain – into the Bay of Bengal. This is the most fertile area of India and one of the most densely populated areas in the world.
3. The Deccan plateau is the large area of raised land between two mountain ranges, the Western and Eastern Ghats, in the south.
4. The dry, sandy Thar Desert in Rajasthan, which covers 260 000 km^2 and is almost twice the size of Bangladesh.

Climate

As India is so huge, the climate varies greatly, but is dominated by monsoon winds. It is warm in most parts of India through the year, but gets very cold in the mountains. It contains some of the driest (the Thar Desert) and the wettest places in the world.

The flag of India

The orange represents the Hindus, the green represents Muslims and the white the hope that the two can live in peace. The blue wheel is an ancient Buddhist symbol which stands for peaceful change. The peacock is the national bird of India.

Languages

India has 16 official languages. Hindi is the main language, and is the fifth most spoken language in the world. Different languages use different alphabets – Hindi using the Devanagari alphabet, Urdu using writing similar to Arabic. English is an official language. There are hundreds of regional dialects.

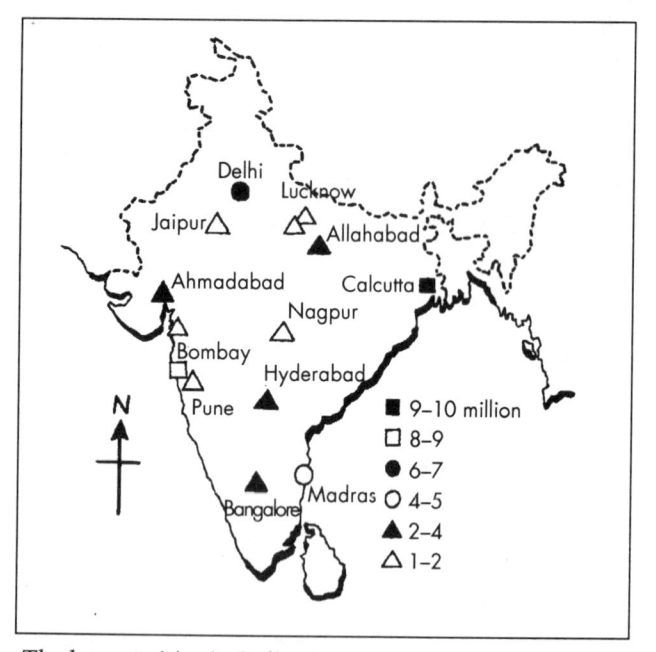

The largest cities in India.

activity sheet 5

Travelling to India

You need
- poster 1
- an atlas

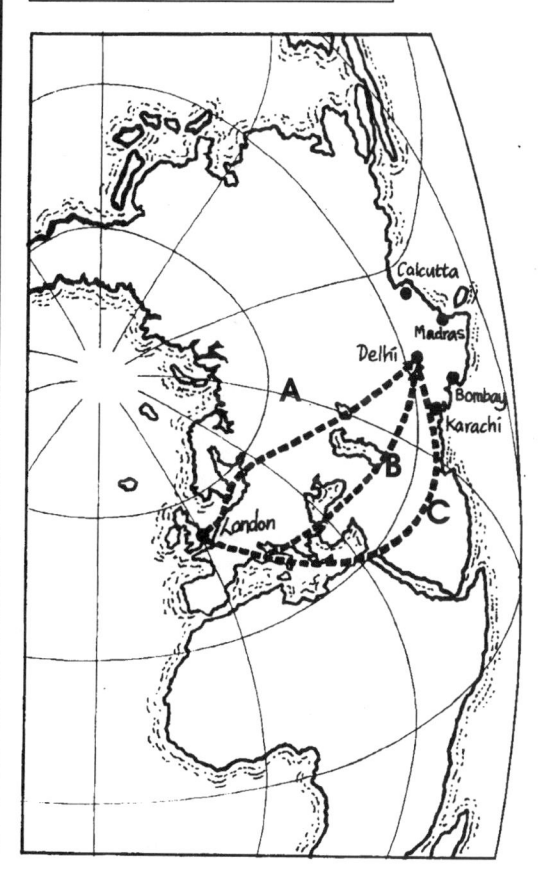

This drawing shows part of the globe. It shows three of the main routes flown by aeroplanes to Delhi in India, from London.

1. Using an atlas to help you, plot each of the six cities on the map below.
   Now draw the three flight routes.

2. What do you notice about route **A** on your flat map?

3. Why do you think routes are shown on maps like the one shown rather than flat maps?

4. You want to give passengers details of the flight. Describe each route, saying which countries and seas you fly over.

5. Label some of the countries on your map.

6. For each route, suggest an airport where the plane might stop to pick up passengers.

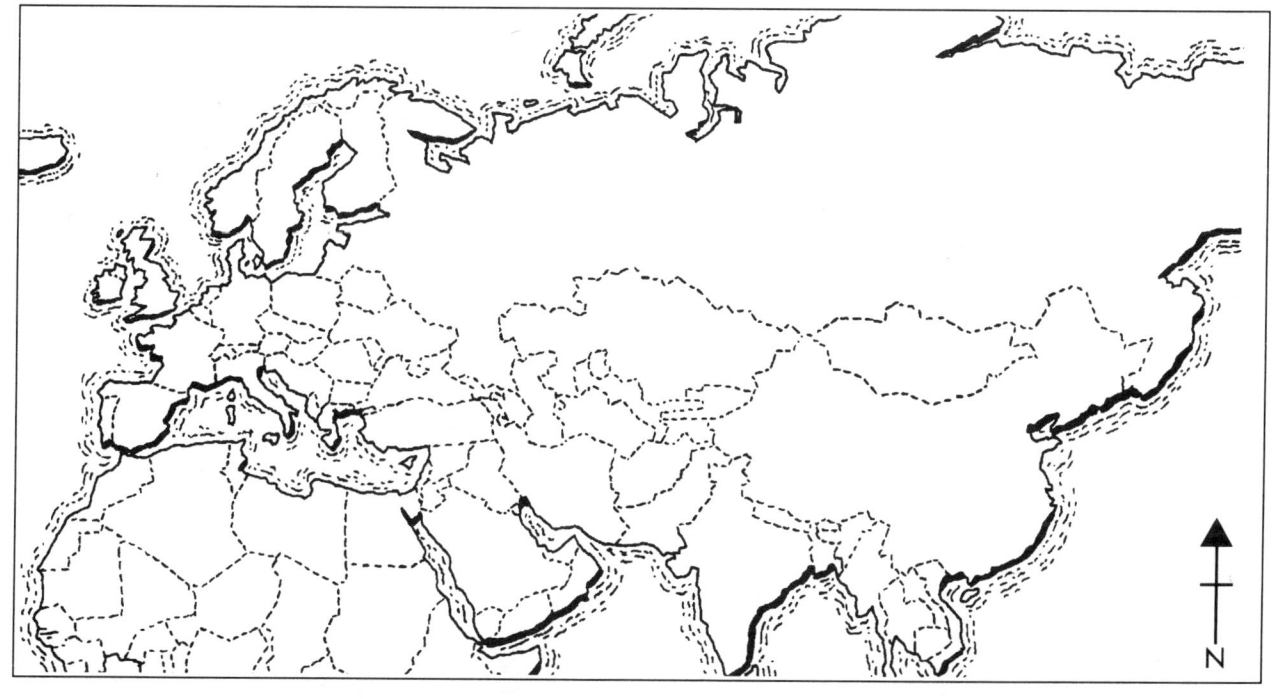

© Folens (copiable page)   FOLENS GEOGRAPHY: An Indian Locality   25

A map of India

You need
- an atlas
- poster 1

- Use an atlas to add details to this map of India.
- Some important cities have been shown for you to name.
- Add the names of the countries around India.
- Name the mountains marked.
- Name the bay to the east of India.
- Name the sea to the west of India.
- Name the ocean which lies to the south.

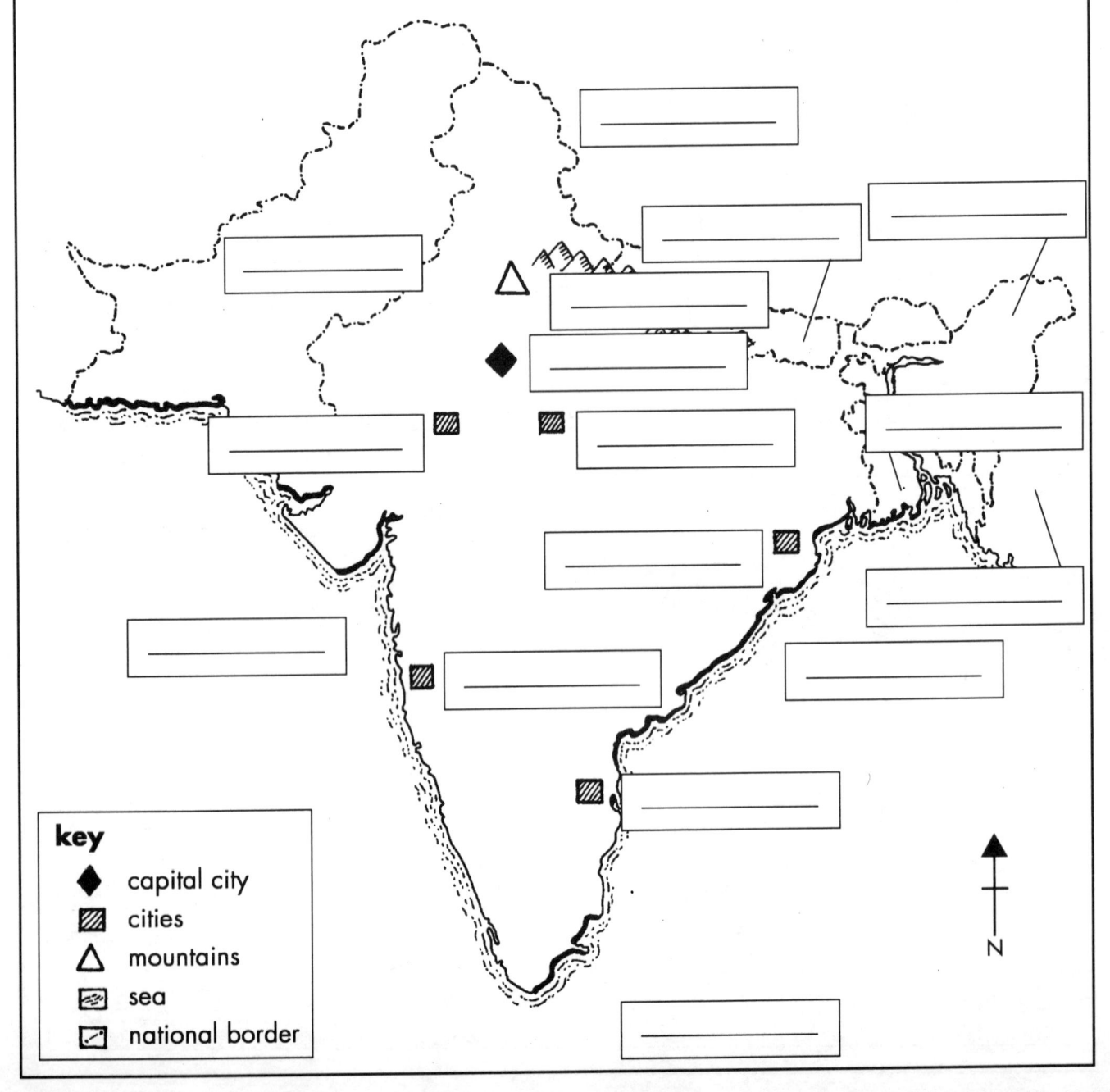

key
- ◆ capital city
- ▨ cities
- △ mountains
- 〰 sea
- ⊡ national border

The landscape of India

India is about thirteen times bigger than the UK. There are many types of landscape – mountains, desert, rainforests and plains, but India can be divided into four different regions:

You need
- an atlas
- poster 1

1. The Himalayan Mountains – where there are the highest mountains in the world.
2. The plain around the River Ganges – where crops are grown and which is one of the most highly populated areas in the world.
3. A plateau (a large area of raised land) between two mountain ranges.
4. The dry, sandy Thar Desert which covers a large part of Rajasthan.

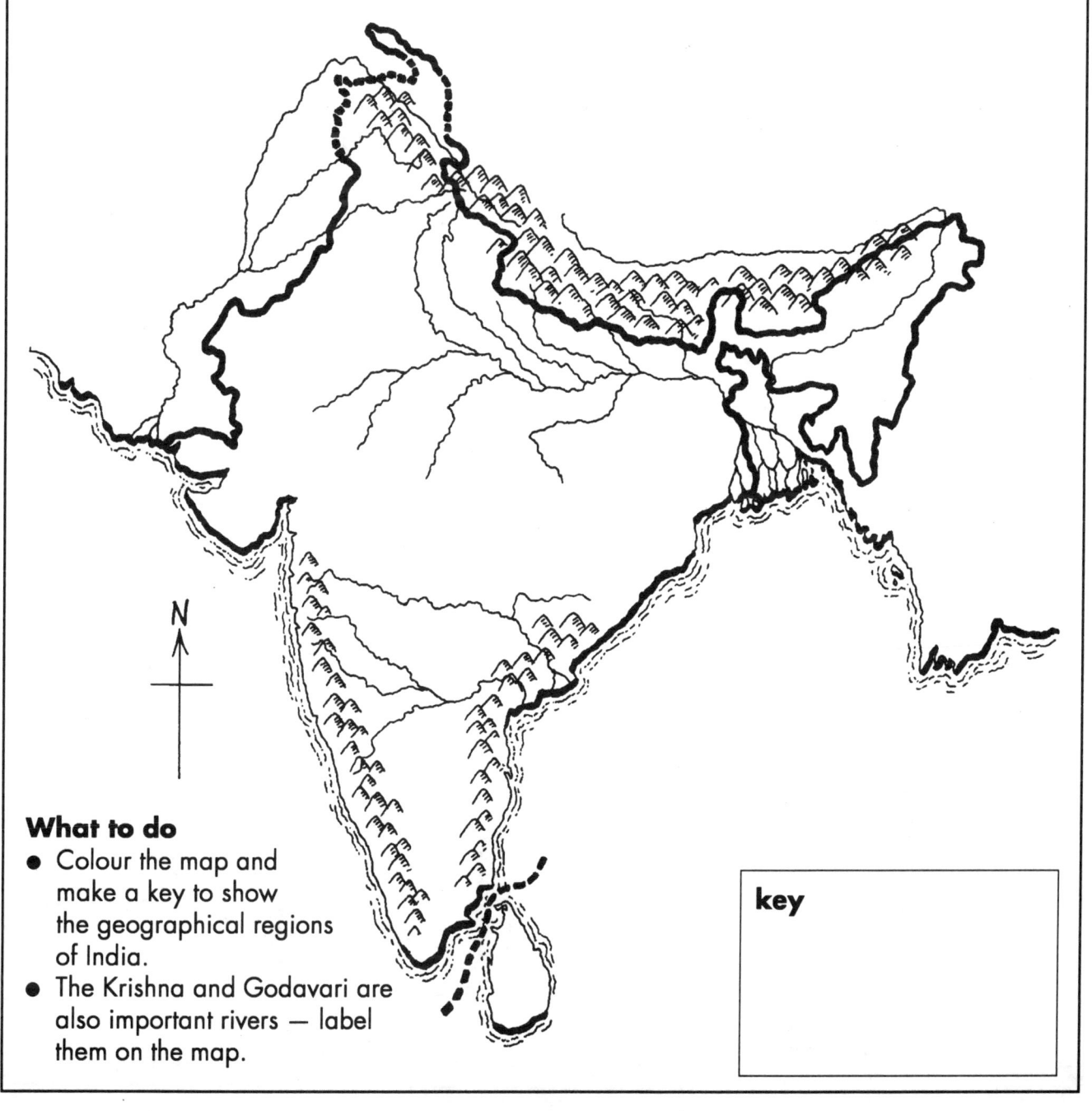

What to do
- Colour the map and make a key to show the geographical regions of India.
- The Krishna and Godavari are also important rivers — label them on the map.

key

pupil information sheet 2

Weather in India

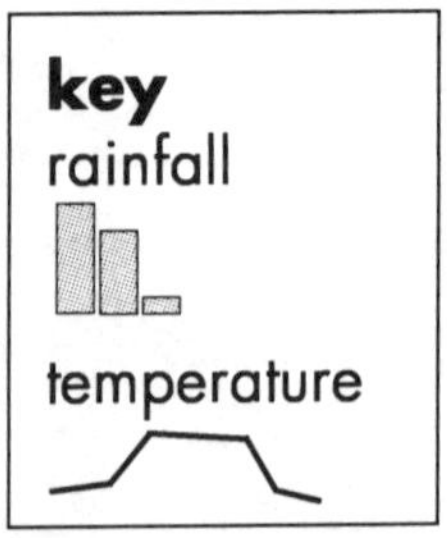

key
rainfall
temperature

These graphs show the average monthly rainfall, measured in millimetres (bar graphs) and the average daily temperatures (line graphs) for five places in India.

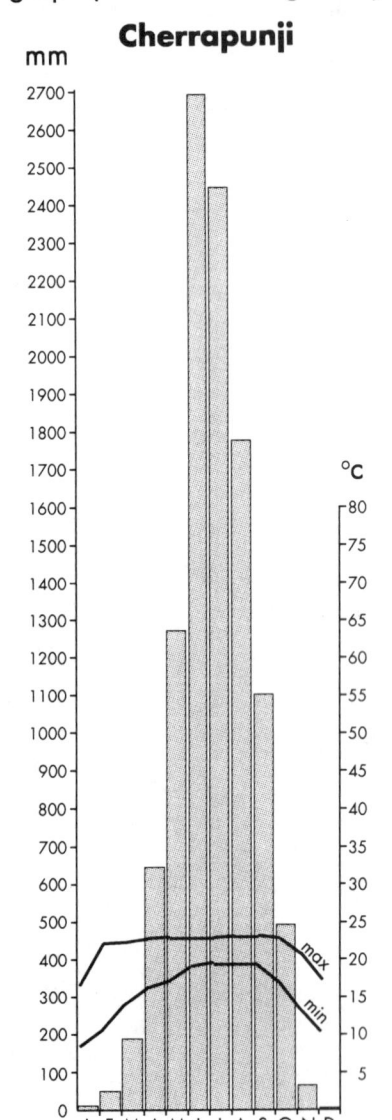

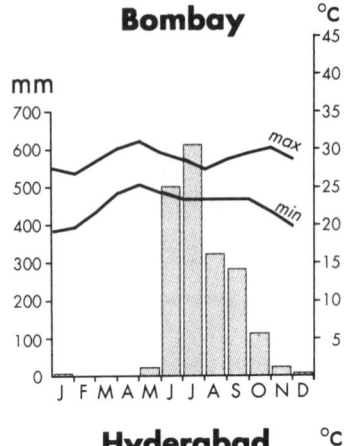

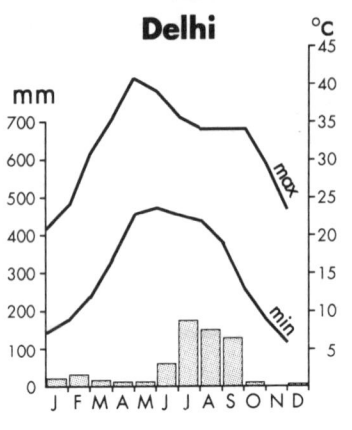

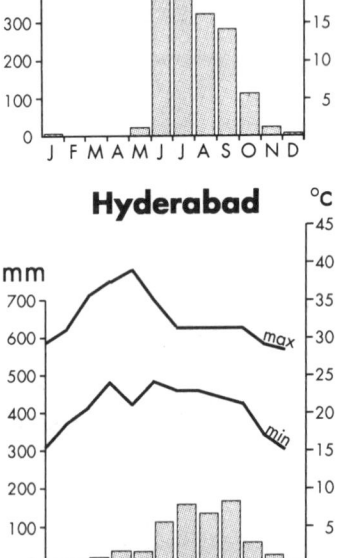

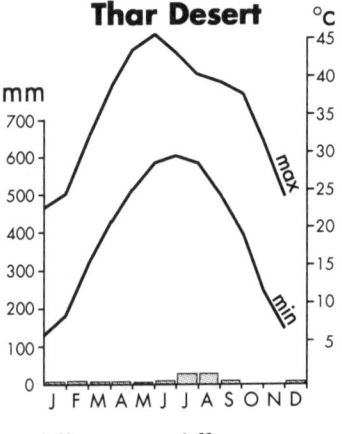

(Graphs shown for: Cherrapunji, Bombay, Delhi, Hyderabad, Thar Desert — each showing monthly rainfall in mm and max/min temperatures in °C across months J F M A M J J A S O N D.)

India is a huge country, so its climate is different in different parts of the country. In the Himalayas, snow falls on the high ground in winter but in the south temperatures can reach 45°C in the summer. The Thar Desert in the west has hardly any rain but in the north east there can be 20 metres of rain a year!

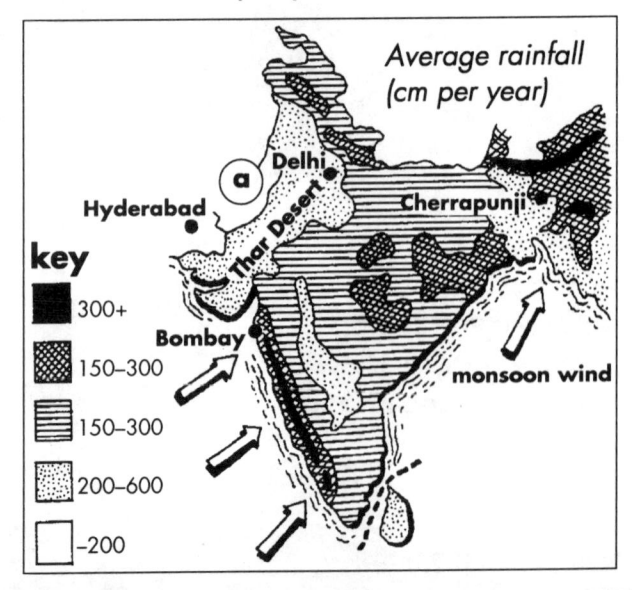

India has three seasons: Winter lasts from October to February when the weather is cool and dry. The weather is hot and dry in Spring, March to May. In Summer, June to September, it is wet and very hot.

Most of the rain falls in one season called the monsoon when it pours down. This rain is very important to the farmers because 70% of India's rain falls in this period. The rain is brought by a wind (the monsoon wind) which blows from the south west, from the equator. It soaks the south of India first then moves across the whole country.

Average rainfall (cm per year)

key
- 300+
- 150–300
- 150–300
- 200–600
- –200

Map of India showing Delhi, Hyderabad, Cherrapunji, Bombay, Thar Desert, and monsoon wind arrows.

FOLENS GEOGRAPHY: *An Indian Locality* © Folens (copiable page)

activity sheet 6

Climate and weather

1. Which are the wettest months of the year in each of these five places?

Place	Month
Thar Desert	
Delhi	
Cherrapunji	
Bombay	
Hyderabad	

You need
- poster 1
- information sheet 2

2. Answer these questions:
   a. Give a reason why Cherrapunji has the most rain.
   _____

   b. Give a reason why Delhi has much less rain.
   _____

3. a. What is the name of the area marked **a** on the map? _____
   b. Why does this area have so little rain? _____
   _____

4. a. Which months do you think are the monsoon periods for each place?
   b. Describe, in the chart, the weather for each of the places in September. Is the weather dry, wet, very wet or monsoon? Is it warm, hot or very hot?

Place	Monsoon months	Weather
Thar Desert		
Delhi		
Cherrapunji		
Bombay		
Hyderabad		

5. a. Which is the hottest place? _____
   b. Give a reason for the high temperatures.

6. a. Which place has the lowest temperatures? _____
   b. Give a reason for your answer. _____
   _____

On the back of this activity sheet answer these questions:

7. Why are the monsoon rains so important for the people in India?

8. What problems do you think might be caused by the monsoon rains?

9. Why do you think the monsoon months are different for each place?

10. When would you choose to visit India? Give a reason for your choice.

Teachers' notes (mask before photocopying)
Draw full size graphs for the classroom wall of the rainfall in each of these five places, and of your own locality, so that children will gain the full impact of the amount of rain which falls in the monsoon season.

© Folens (copiable page)   FOLENS GEOGRAPHY: An Indian Locality

activity sheet 7

Weather: comparing capital cities

London

	Highest temp °C	Lowest temp °C	Average rainfall (mm)
Jan	6	2	54
Feb	7	2	40
Mar	10	3	37
Apr	13	6	37
May	17	8	46
June	20	12	45
July	22	14	57
Aug	21	13	59
Sept	19	11	49
Oct	14	8	57
Nov	10	5	64
Dec	7	4	48

Delhi

	Highest temp °C	Lowest temp °C	Average rainfall (mm)
Jan	21	7	20
Feb	24	9	30
Mar	31	14	15
Apr	36	20	10
May	41	26	10
June	39	28	70
July	36	27	180
Aug	34	26	160
Sept	34	24	130
Oct	34	18	10
Nov	29	11	0
Dec	23	8	5

1. Draw a bar graph like this that shows the average monthly rainfall for London and Delhi throughout the year. Look carefully at the figures before you choose your scale.

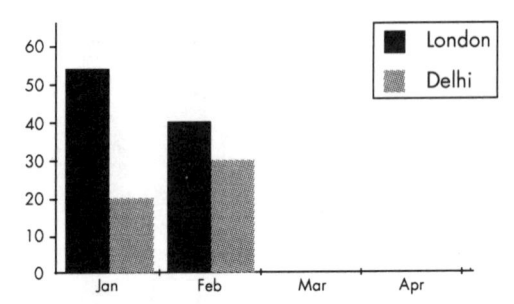

2. In which months do you think monsoon winds blow over Delhi?

3. In which months is Delhi drier than London?

4. Write a sentence about the pattern of rainfall in each city during the year.

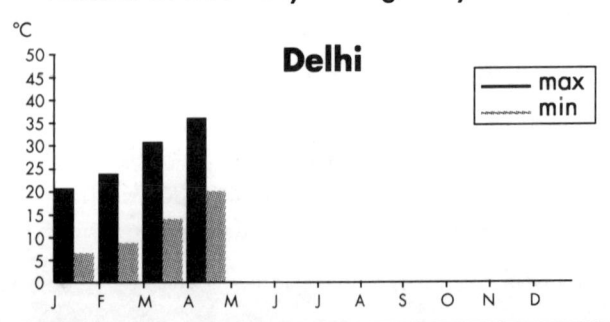

5. Draw line graphs like the one shown of Delhi to show the maximum and minimum temperatures for Delhi and London.

6. Compare the two graphs and write some sentences about what you notice.

7. Here are the figures for Jodhpur in Rajasthan. Find figures for your locality so that you can compare your weather with the weather in Jodhpur.

Jodhpur

	Highest temp °C	Lowest temp °C	Average rainfall (mm)
Jan	25	9	7
Feb	28	12	5
Mar	33	17	2
Apr	38	22	2
May	42	27	6
June	40	29	31
July	36	27	122
Aug	33	25	145
Sept	35	24	47
Oct	36	20	7
Nov	31	14	3
Dec	27	11	1

FOLENS GEOGRAPHY: An Indian Locality © Folens (copiable page)

activity sheet 8

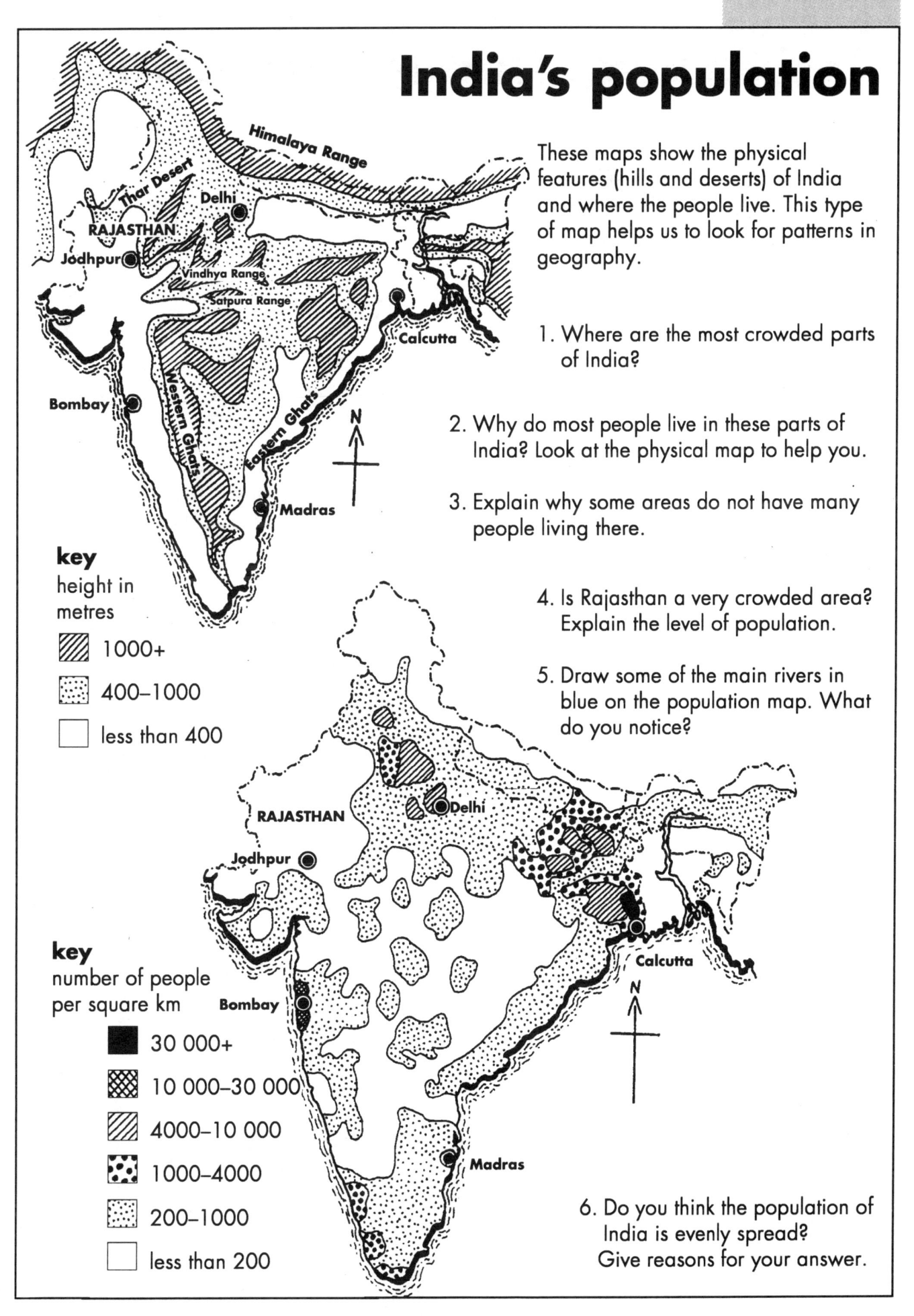

India's population

These maps show the physical features (hills and deserts) of India and where the people live. This type of map helps us to look for patterns in geography.

1. Where are the most crowded parts of India?

2. Why do most people live in these parts of India? Look at the physical map to help you.

3. Explain why some areas do not have many people living there.

4. Is Rajasthan a very crowded area? Explain the level of population.

5. Draw some of the main rivers in blue on the population map. What do you notice?

6. Do you think the population of India is evenly spread? Give reasons for your answer.

key
height in metres
- 1000+
- 400–1000
- less than 400

key
number of people per square km
- 30 000+
- 10 000–30 000
- 4000–10 000
- 1000–4000
- 200–1000
- less than 200

© Folens (copiable page)   FOLENS GEOGRAPHY: An Indian Locality   31

map 3

Train travel through Rajasthan

key
- Broad gauge single line
- Broad gauge double line
- Metre gauge single line
- Metre gauge double line
- Electrified
- State/Union border

32 FOLENS GEOGRAPHY: An Indian Locality © Folens (copiable page)

Train travel

You need
- map 3
- poster 5

1. Find two routes through Rajasthan from Ahmadabad to Delhi. List four stops on each route.

Route A	Route B
Ahmadabad	Ahmadabad
Delhi	Delhi

2. Find two routes through Rajasthan from Udaipur City to Jaipur. List four stops on each route.

Route A	Route B
Udaipur City	Udaipur City
Jaipur	Jaipur

3. List four railway junctions (towns where different lines meet).

   a. _____   c. _____

   b. _____   d. _____

Look at the train timetable.

4. How long does it take:

   a. From Delhi to Jaipur? _____

   b. From Jaipur to Ajmer? _____

   c. From Ajmer to Udaipur? _____

5. How long is the journey time from Delhi to Udaipur?

   _____

PINK CITY EXPRESS TIMETABLE	
Delhi	0600
Rewari Junction	0730
Alwar	0914
Bandikui Junction	1015
Jaipur	1150
Ajmer	1430
Bhilwara	1717
Chittaurgarh	1830
Udaipur	2210

pupil information sheet 3

Industries in India

Where do people work?   What do they make?   What do they grow?

Many people in India are unemployed, or only work part-time.
Where are the workers employed?

	Males	Females	Total
agriculture, forestry, fishing	139.4m	52.0m	191.4m
services	24.0m	5.3m	29.3m
manufacturing	24.0m	4.7m	28.7m
trade – buying, selling	19.9m	1.4m	21.3m
transport	7.8m	0.2m	8.0m
building	5.1m	0.4m	5.5m
mining	1.5m	0.2m	1.7m

In agriculture, what do people produce?
(measured in tonnes)

Food
sugar cane	260.0m
rice	81.3m
wheat	65.2m
maize	9.3m
ground nuts	8.6m
millet	7.1m
rapeseed	6.3m

Other
cotton lint	11.8m
jute	8.3m

In industry, what do people make?

bicycles	8.9m
electric fans	6.5m
motor bikes, scooters	1.2m
diesel engines	1.8m
sewing machines	0.1m

Other main products

aluminium	cement
cotton/cloth	petroleum products
fertilisers	refined sugar

Which animal products are most used?
(measured in tonnes)

buffaloes' milk	31.7m
cows' milk	30.5m
goats' milk	2.4m
beef and veal	1.3m
buffalo meat	1.2m

What do people mine?
(measured in tonnes)

coal	524.6m
limestone	88.6m
iron ore	60.8m
crude petroleum	32.2m

Products not measured in tonnes

diamonds
copper
gold
natural gas

What do people fish for? (measured in tonnes)

sea fish	2.7m

(main fish caught are Bombay duck, croakers and drums, shrimps, anchovies and sardines)

freshwater fish	2.0m

Teachers' notes (mask before photocopying)
These facts are intended to be used for creating graphs for drawing conclusions and then discussion, and for use with activity sheet 10.
The figures given are for one year's production (1995). Collect figures from the UK (local library world atlas book) and compare.

FOLENS GEOGRAPHY: *An Indian Locality*

activity sheet 10

Trade and industry

These graphs show how much India earned from selling products to other countries (exports) and how much India spent on buying things from other countries (imports) in one year.

You need
- information sheet 3

Imports

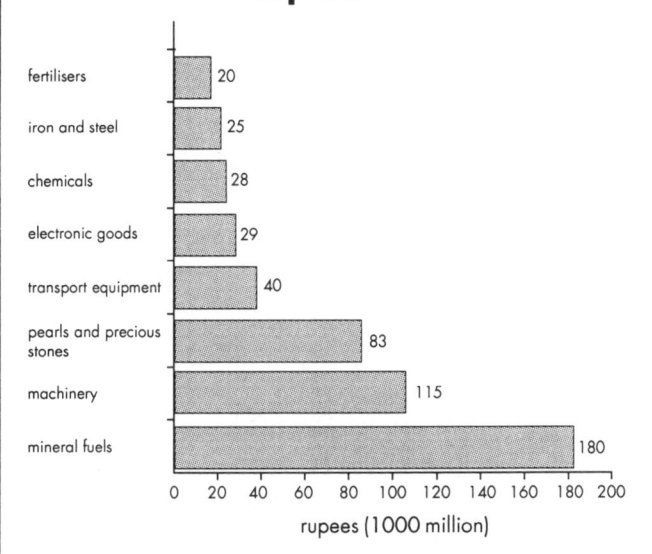

	rupees (1000 million)
fertilisers	20
iron and steel	25
chemicals	28
electronic goods	29
transport equipment	40
pearls and precious stones	83
machinery	115
mineral fuels	180

Exports

	rupees (1000 million)
oil	23
marine products	26
leather	41
chemicals	46
material (cotton)	48
clothes	81
engineering products	85
gems and jewellery	125

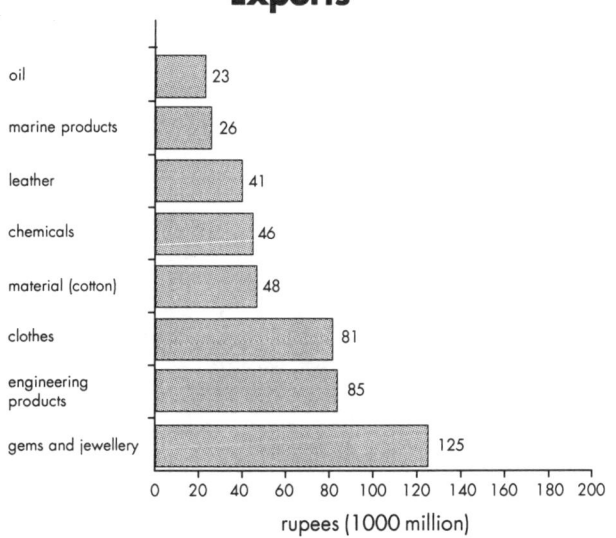

The graphs show the main products which earned the most money and which India spent the most money on.

Altogether India spent 731 010 million rupees on imports. India earned 697 510 million rupees from exports.

1. What does India earn the most money from?

2. List three things which Indian factories make which are mostly sold in India (they are not important exports). Why do you think that they are not exported? Give a reason for each of your choices.

3. What things are made by people to sell abroad?

4. What does India need the most from other countries?

5. Examine the graphs and the figures on the information page carefully. Name two things India needs to buy from abroad that it does not produce enough of in its own country.

6. Notice that most of the workers in India work in agriculture, but products from agriculture are not an important export. Give a reason why.

7. Why do you think so many people work on the land?

© Folens (copiable page)   FOLENS GEOGRAPHY: An Indian Locality   35

pupil information sheet 4
Religion in India

Here is some information about the way people worship in India. This will help you to understand more about the way people live in places like Rajasthan.
The key words are printed in dark print – you might like to find out more by using these in your library or from CD Rom.

Religion is very important in India. People have different ways of life – often because of their religion and what they believe. Many different religions are followed. This pie chart shows that most people are **Hindus**.

Hindus believe in one god called Brahman the Creator who takes the form of many other gods and goddesses. The main ones are **Brahma**, **Vishnu** and **Shiva**.

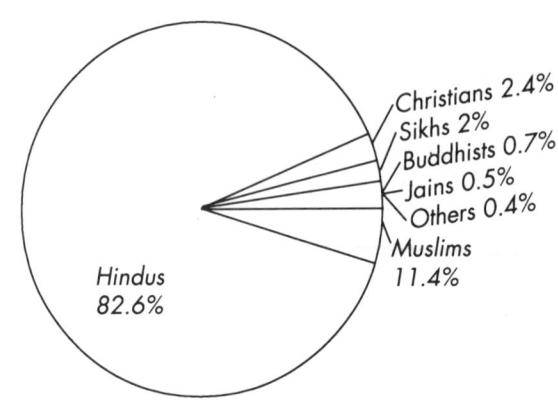

Pie chart: Hindus 82.6%, Muslims 11.4%, Christians 2.4%, Sikhs 2%, Buddhists 0.7%, Jains 0.5%, Others 0.4%

Hindus worship in many different ways. They pray to statues of their gods in **shrines** at home. Some people visit a **temple** and take offerings of flowers or food. Hindus aim to lead good lives because they believe that they are reborn after death (**reincarnation**); a good person will return to a better life.

Traditionally, Hindus in India have been divided into four groups (classes or **castes**). These were based on the kinds of jobs people did long ago. The highest caste was the **Brahmin** (priests), then came Kshatriyas (soldiers and noblemen). There were then Vaishyas (merchants and traders) and Shudras (craftsmen and servants). Millions of others were called '**untouchables**' who did jobs like cleaning the streets. Laws have been passed to prevent the worst effects of the caste system but it has been a tradition for so long that it still affects people's lives.

About one-tenth of Indians are **Muslims** who follow the religion of **Islam**. They believe in one god, called **Allah**, and in his prophet, **Muhammad**. Pakistan and Bangladesh, India's neighbours, are both Muslim countries. Muslims worship in **mosques**, and pray five times a day.

The **Sikh** religion was started in India almost 500 years ago, by **Guru Nanak**. They worship in temples called **Gurdwaras** and believe in tolerance for all. **Buddhist** and **Jain** religions are very old religions, starting in India about 500BC. The Buddhists follow the teachings of **Buddha**. Buddhists and Jains believe that they must not harm any living thing.

Teachers' notes (mask before photocopying)
This is meant as a starting point for discussion or further research by the children. Some background information is needed for an understanding of the way of life in Jodhpur; see pages 56–58 about the school children and pages 50 and 54 on the development of the locality. Research on religious festivals would also be very useful – as they are an important feature in the lives of the communities throughout Rajasthan.

Rajasthan

Background information

Regions
Rajasthan covers 342 274km^2 and divides into two geographical regions – the south-eastern hills (the Aravalli Hills) which is a fertile area of forests and irrigated valleys, and the great Thar Desert which gets virtually no rain.
There is evidence to suggest that even the western and northern areas were not always desert. Elephants once lived in this area but now forests have been replaced by sand dunes, and elephants by camels – due partly to the influence of humans.

The population
In a country with a vast population and overcrowded cities, Rajasthan is one area where people can find space, yet it has one of the world's highest birth rates. It has a population of approximately 52 million people, of which 17% once belonged to the 'untouchables' caste and 12% are tribal people and nomads.

It is one of the poorest and most backward states in India, the average income being two-thirds of that of India as a whole. The average literacy rate is only 24%. In some tourist areas such as Jaisalmer and Barmer the female literacy rate is virtually non-existent. This is reflected in some social customs such as child marriage which continues despite laws against it. Recent estimates put child marriages at 50 000 per year in Rajasthan. Arranged marriages are the norm.

Economy
Rajasthan still has relatively little manufacturing industry, but it is beginning to develop, especially in the production of cement, electrical equipment, trucks and tractors. Many workers still have traditional craft workshops, producing carpets, jewellery and fabrics. There is some mining for marble, quartz, silver and gemstones. It is mainly an agricultural area where people provide their own food with some to sell as a source of income.

Rajasthan produces nearly 40% of India's wool and a large number of rural people are involved in sheep rearing. Rajasthan is just beginning to grow cash crops for export, such as sugar. This has developed as a result of irrigation schemes such as the Indira Gandhi Canal – a 649km canal starting in the Punjab, with 9000km of tributaries, running through the Thar Desert. It is helping to prevent the expansion of the desert and allows new crops to be grown.

Although industrial and educational facilities have developed, their impact has been limited by the great increase in population.

Tourism
One of the biggest industries in Rajasthan is tourism. Visitors are attracted in large numbers because of the rich history – and vivid culture. The state is almost an 'open air museum'. Recently places such as Pushkar have been added to the 'hippy' route which has increased numbers of tourists and caused conflict with locals.

History
Civilisation came to Rajasthan with the Harappa culture (2500BC) – the Indus Valley civilisation. It was historically an area of small republics with tribal wars, AD647 to 1200 being dominated by the Rajputs who belonged to the Kshatriya (warrior ruler caste). Until 1950 the state was known as Rajputana – 'the country of the Rajputs'.

The Moguls (Mughals) brought a more settled period until the eighteenth century when the British began to take control. It was in this period that many palaces, fortresses and market towns were built.

Following independence, the new government of India made it attractive for the Hindu princes to join with India, rather than Pakistan which was mainly Muslim. The 22 princely states merged into one administrative unit. Many of Rajasthan's ex-princes turned to business – some converting their palaces into luxury hotels (such as the Umaid Bhavan Palace at Jodhpur and the Lake Palace at Udaipur).

activity sheet 11

Rajasthan – map work

You need
- tourist map of Rajasthan

While staying in Jodhpur you visit the fort at Pokaran, the temples and Peacock Island at Osiyan and the desert city of Nagaur.

1. Use the scale on the map to calculate the distance you would need to travel by road to each of these sites, and the direction you would travel.

	direction	**distance**
Pokaran	_____	_____ km
Osiyan	_____	_____ km
Nagaur	_____	_____ km

2. Choose three other places of interest for tourists (use the key) and work out the distances and direction by road from Jodhpur.

	direction	**distance**
_____	_____	_____ km
_____	_____	_____ km
_____	_____	_____ km

3. Grid references help you to locate places on a map. Look closely at the faint blue lines on your map – the grid reference of Jodhpur is (730, 263) – the bottom left-hand corner of the grid square.
   Give the grid references for these cities in Rajasthan:

   Jaisalmer (,   )   Udaipur (,   )
   Jaipur   (,   )   Bikaner (,   )

4. Which District Headquarters will you find in grid squares:

   (71°,25°) _____   (76°,24°) _____   (75°,28°) _____ ?

5. Which country lies to the north west of Rajasthan? _____

6. Which state of India lies to the south west? _____

FOLENS GEOGRAPHY: *An Indian Locality*

activity sheet 12

The physical features of Rajasthan

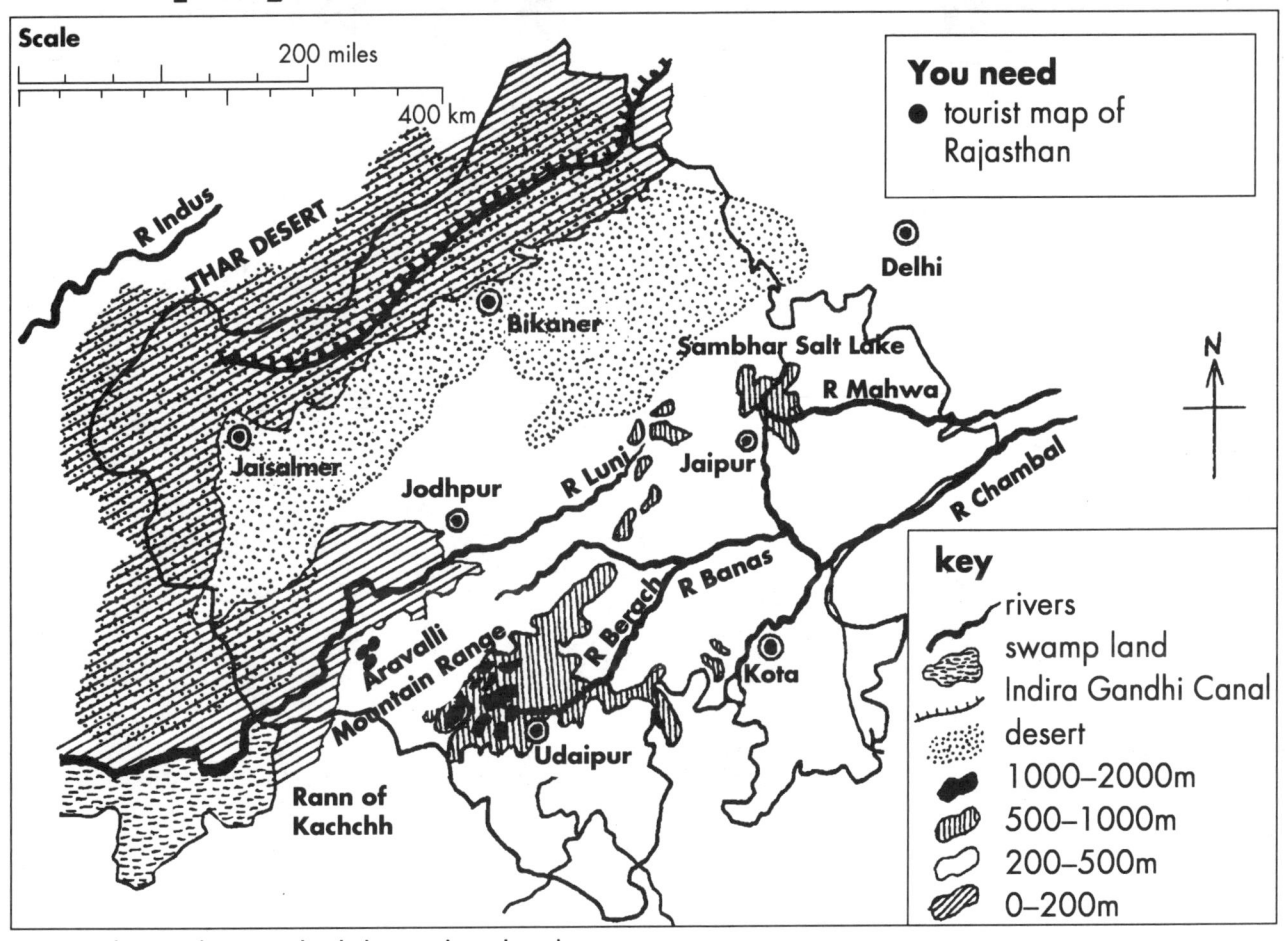

Scale 200 miles / 400 km

You need
- tourist map of Rajasthan

key
- rivers
- swamp land
- Indira Gandhi Canal
- desert
- 1000–2000m
- 500–1000m
- 200–500m
- 0–200m

1. List three places which lie within the desert.

_____   _____   _____

Add some more desert towns to this map.

2. Name a mountain range in Rajasthan. _____

3. Which river flows past Jodhpur? _____

4. Where is its source? _____

5. Where does it flow to? _____

6. The Rann of Kachchh is inland. What kind of land is it? _____

7. Where has a major canal been built? Suggest a reason why it was built in this area.

_____

8. Would you describe Rajasthan as a highland or lowland area of India? _____

© Folens (copiable page)   FOLENS GEOGRAPHY: *An Indian Locality*

pupil information sheet 5

On holiday in Rajasthan

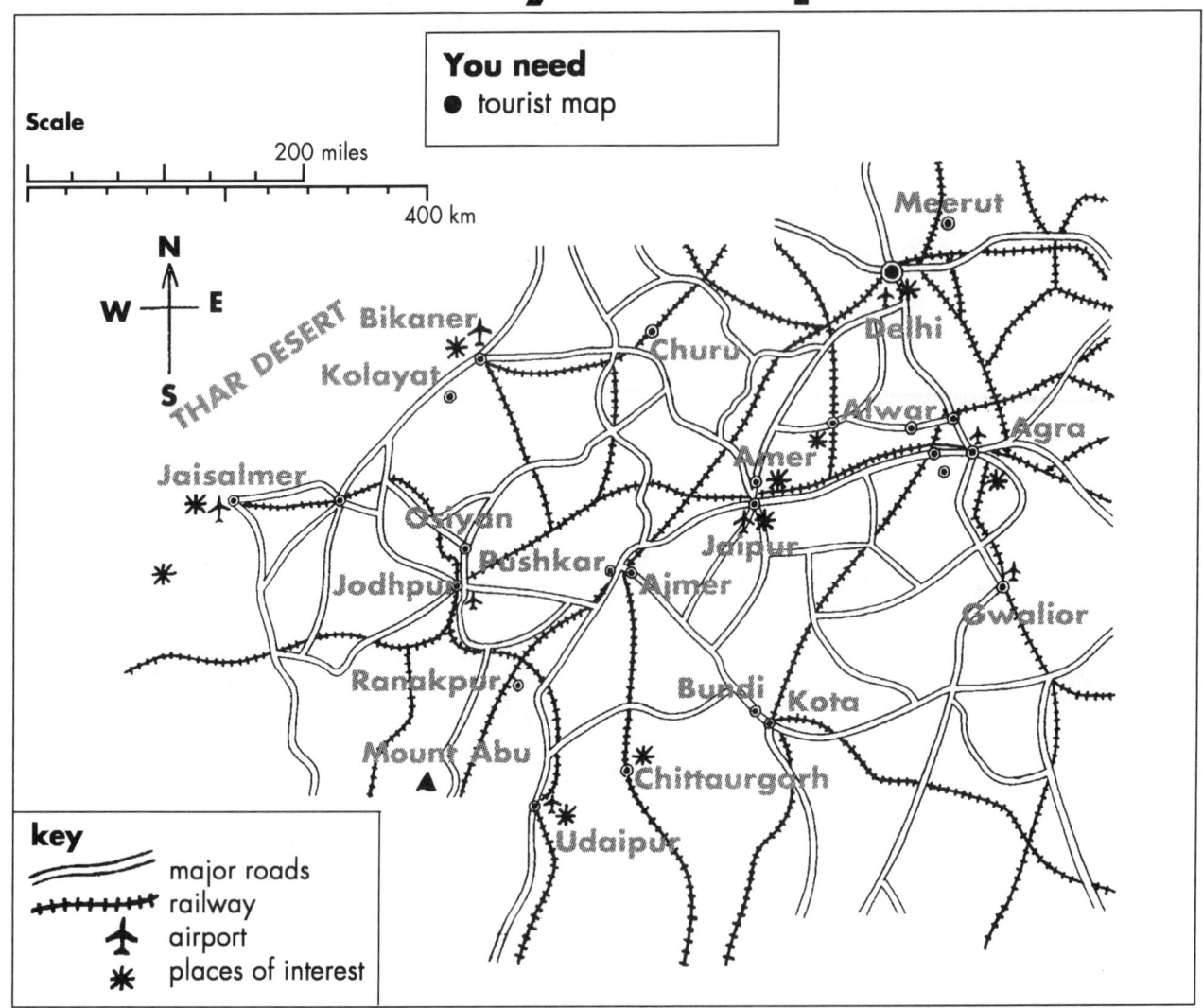

You need
- tourist map

Scale 200 miles / 400 km

key
- major roads
- railway
- ✈ airport
- ✳ places of interest

Distances in kilometres between towns

	Agra	Bikaner	Chittaurgarh	Delhi	Jaipur	Jaisalmer	Jodhpur	Udaipur
Agra	–	584	579	200	230	910	573	604
Bikaner	584	–	611	538	354	326	242	577
Chittaurgarh	579	611	–	583	322	657	372	112
Delhi	200	538	583	–	261	864	604	635
Jaipur	230	354	322	261	–	680	343	374
Jaisalmer	910	326	657	864	680	–	330	665
Jodhpur	573	242	372	604	343	330	–	305
Udaipur	604	577	112	635	374	665	305	–

Most visitors to Rajasthan will arrive in India at the airport in Delhi.

The Taj Mahal at Agra, just outside Rajasthan, is a must for most visitors.

FOLENS GEOGRAPHY: *An Indian Locality*

activity sheet 13

On holiday in Rajasthan

You need
- map 4
- information sheet 5

You are going on holiday to Rajasthan. Your aeroplane lands at Indira Gandhi International Airport in Delhi.

You have planned a week of travel to visit interesting sights in Rajasthan, before staying for a week's holiday in Jodhpur.

The Red Fort.

Here are the places which you have planned to visit:

The Taj Mahal at Agra (just outside Rajasthan)

The forts at Amer (Amber Fort), Bikaner and Jaisalmer

Palaces at Bharatpur, Udaipur and Jaipur

The sacred lake and only temple to Brahma in India, at Pushkar, near Ajmer

The temple at Ranakpur

The Seriska Tiger Reserve near Alwar

The desert by camel

- Decide which of these places you will visit on your journey and which you will visit from Jodhpur.
- Copy and complete the charts below to show your holiday plan.

1st week

from	to	travel by	distance	to visit
Delhi	Agra	train	200km	The Taj Mahal

2nd week

from	to	travel by	distance	to visit
Jodhpur				
Jodhpur				
Jodhpur				

© Folens (copiable page)   FOLENS GEOGRAPHY: *An Indian Locality*   41

activity sheet 14

A tourist in Rajasthan

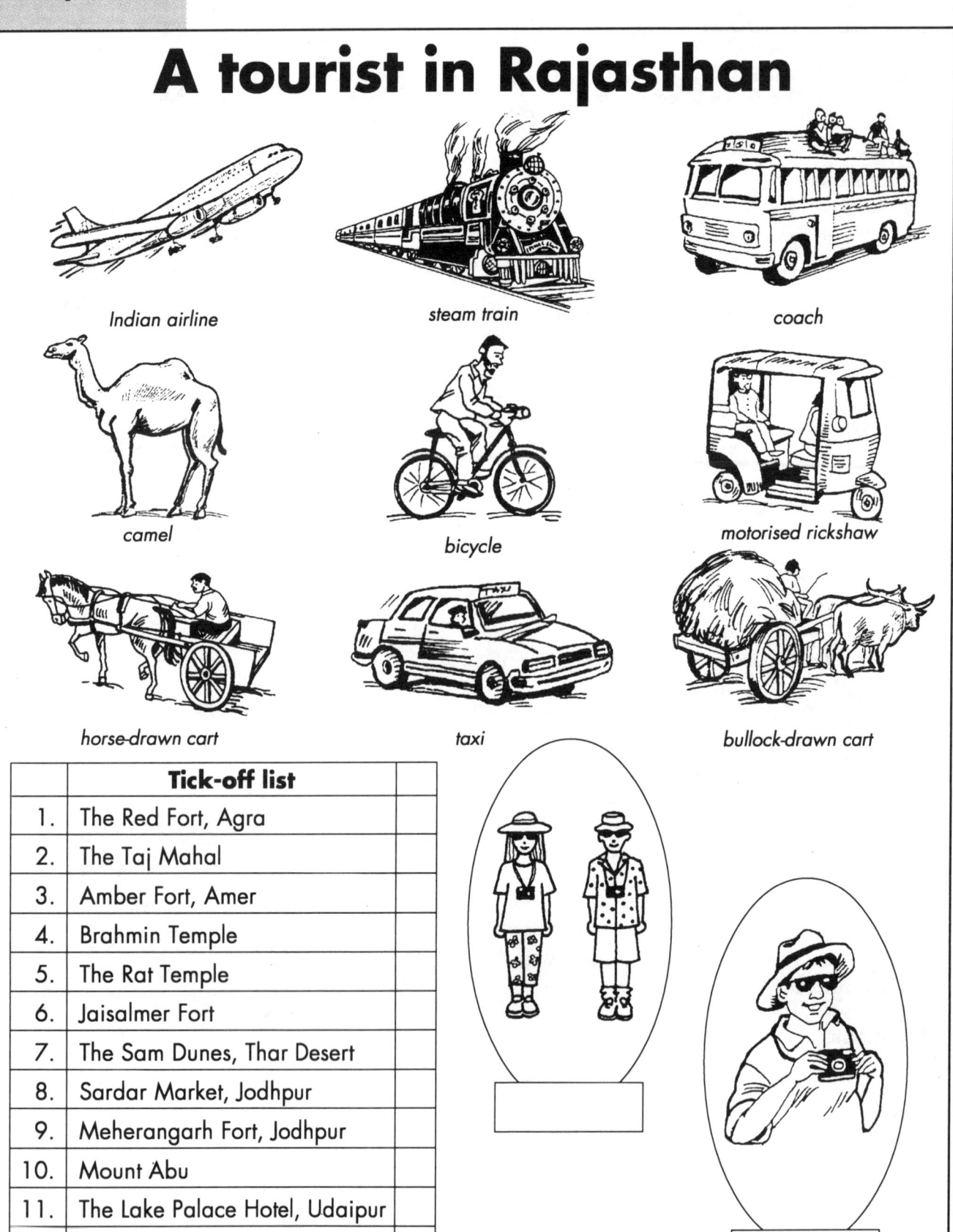

Indian airline *steam train* *coach*

camel *bicycle* *motorised rickshaw*

horse-drawn cart *taxi* *bullock-drawn cart*

	Tick-off list	
1.	The Red Fort, Agra	
2.	The Taj Mahal	
3.	Amber Fort, Amer	
4.	Brahmin Temple	
5.	The Rat Temple	
6.	Jaisalmer Fort	
7.	The Sam Dunes, Thar Desert	
8.	Sardar Market, Jodhpur	
9.	Meherangarh Fort, Jodhpur	
10.	Mount Abu	
11.	The Lake Palace Hotel, Udaipur	
12.	Tigers at Ranthambhore National Park	

Teachers' notes (mask before photocopying)
Photocopy the map, enlarging to A3 (one per group).
Make three copies of the transport pictures – these would be better mounted on card. Turn them face down on the table.
Each player needs a tick-off list and a figure to move. The figures can be mounted on card. Use a cross-piece support or modelling clay to stand them on the map.

42 FOLENS GEOGRAPHY: *An Indian Locality* © Folens (copiable page)

map 4

A tourist in Rajasthan

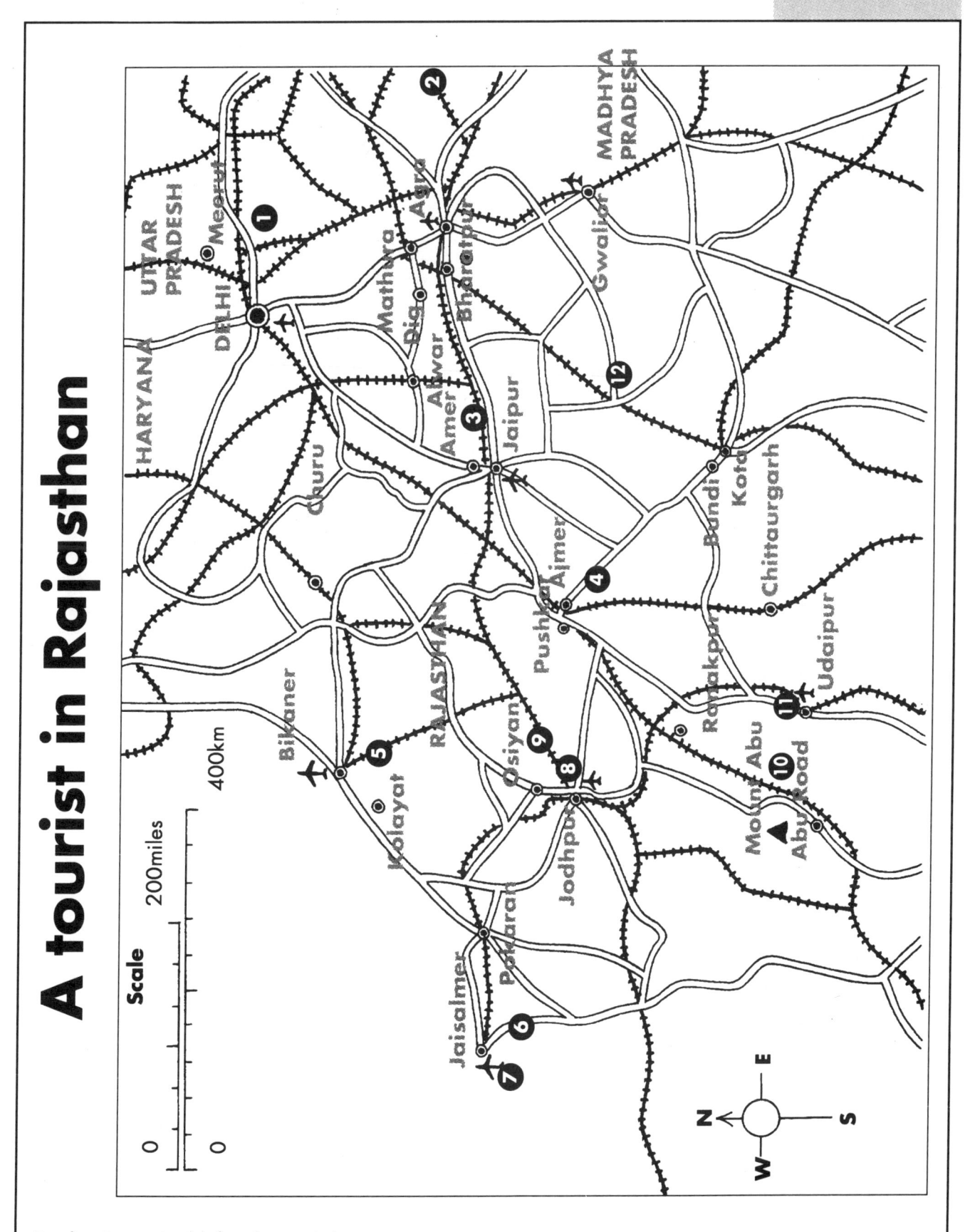

Teachers' notes (mask before photocopying)
Playing the game
The aim of the game is to see all the places on the tick-off list (activity sheet 14). Players begin by turning over a transport card. All players start from Delhi airport. They can visit sites in any order. A player moves by turning over a transport card (for example, if it is a plane the player can fly to another destination), or they can stay until a suitable card is turned over. On landing at the airport, or arriving at the station, another transport type (rickshaw, cart, taxi) should be used to get to the attraction. Players can be challenged by others at any time (for example, if they choose to travel 300km by camel!) then they must justify to the group why they have chosen it.

© Folens (copiable page)   FOLENS GEOGRAPHY: *An Indian Locality*   43

Farming

Notes for teachers

Farms
The whole of the Indian subcontinent supports a mainly agricultural way of life. More than two-thirds of the people work on the land and depend on agriculture for their living. Most farms, however, are tiny. Only a few people own more than ten hectares of land. This small area of land has to provide food for both the family and to sell to provide some income. Those who have no land often work on other people's farms.

Crops
Of the available farm land, three-quarters is used for growing crops. The main crops are rice and wheat, which provide the main element of people's diets. Pulses, chickpeas, lentils and beans are also grown. Jute, cotton, sugar cane and tea are grown mainly for export (cash crops).

India is the world's largest producer of tea. Since independence, production of wheat, rice and pulses has increased so much that India is now self sufficient in these crops. In case the harvest fails, 20 million tonnes of grain is kept in reserve by the government.

Water management
The vast majority of farms depend on monsoon rains for water – only a fifth of farms get water from irrigation projects. If the monsoon fails or heavy rains cause floods, farmers can face hunger and ruin. Over the centuries different methods have been developed to make the best of local environmental conditions.

In Rajasthan, dam-like structures (johads) are built along contour lines. These trap the monsoon rains before they run off the surface, causing soil erosion. The water soaks into the land, raising the water-table and so refilling the wells. An ambitious project to take water to the Thar Desert in Rajasthan has also been developed. The Indira Gandhi Canal carries water from the Himalayas as far as Jaisalmer.

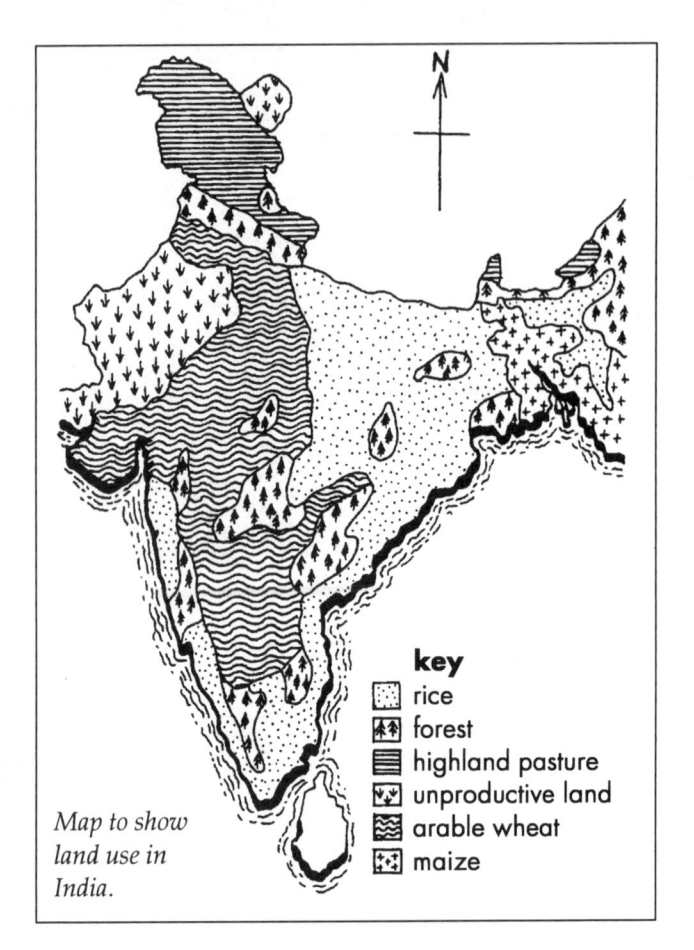

Map to show land use in India.

key
- rice
- forest
- highland pasture
- unproductive land
- arable wheat
- maize

Animals
The cow, a holy and protected animal, is essential to farming in India. India has the largest population of cattle in the world. They plough, haul, thresh crops and raise water from the wells. Dried cattle dung is used for fuel and, mixed with mud, as a building material. There are also many buffaloes, sheep and goats. Where there is not much pasture land, such as in Rajasthan, there is overgrazing and this leads to desertification – dusty wastes instead of farm land.

Unemployment
With the growth in population, particularly in the countryside, the number of rural workers has increased but the amount of land and the number of jobs has stayed the same. This has led to unemployment and underemployment, as agricultural jobs are dependent on the weather – if the monsoon fails or washes away the crops there is no work. Recent census figures showed that approximately 6% of agricultural workers were unemployed but including the underemployed this figure was nearer 23%, meaning that 44 million men were not earning a full wage.

Life in rural Rajasthan

The population of Rajasthan is getting bigger and much of the area is desert. This diagram shows what has happened as farmers divide up their plots of land for their children.

As the land is divided, each farmer has a smaller piece of land and so produces less food, only enough for the family and not enough to sell. To produce more he will need to buy machinery or new crops. Many farmers in Rajasthan cannot afford to do this.

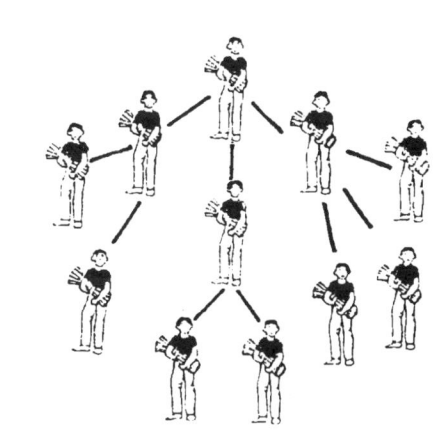

1. What will happen if this continues? _____

_____

Here are some problems faced by the farmers in Rajasthan. How do you think they will affect the farmer's family? In groups, discuss what the consequences might be.

Problems	Consequences
The land is not good, many crops die.	
The monsoon rains wash away the crops.	
A factory opens in Jodhpur, offering work to those who move there.	
Disease strikes the village and many of the animals die.	
Young people do not want to work on the farm, life is more exciting in the towns.	
Farmers can't afford to buy machines.	
A tributary from the Indira Gandhi canal is built to the village.	

pupil information sheet 6

Deserts

A large part of Rajasthan is covered by the Thar Desert. The land has many large sand dunes, but also some rock and scrub land (small plants).

What is a desert?
A desert, like the Thar Desert, is a place that gets less than 25cm of rain each year. Near the tropics they are places where wind blows away the clouds, making the area very hot, but also often cold at night. Not all deserts are hot – further north there are dry cold areas.

Wind blows over a mound.

The top gradually builds up to a point.

Eventually this collapses.

Dunes
The Sam Dunes in the Thar Desert are a popular place for tourists to visit. Dunes are made by the wind carrying sand for short distances. When something (such as a plant or a rock) gets in the way, the wind slows down and the sand is dropped. As the pile of dropped sand gets bigger, a bigger obstacle is made and more sand is dropped.

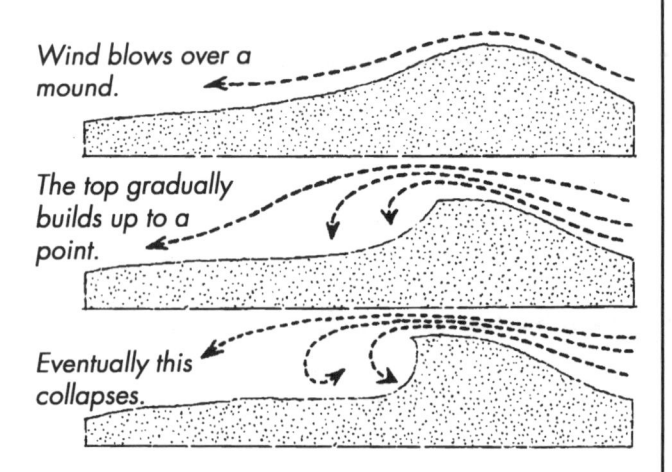

Desertification
This part of Rajasthan was not always desert. There were trees and plants. People lived here growing food in the time of the Indus Valley civilisation. There is less rainfall now than 3000 years ago but too much farming and cutting down of trees can ruin the land. Because of overgrazing there are not enough plants to keep the dust on the ground and help dew to form, so the land is becoming drier and drier. This makes the land turn to desert – called desertification – and this is what is happening at the moment in Rajasthan. If grasses are allowed to grow, with water brought by the Indira Gandhi Canal, parts of the desert can be reclaimed.

The ship of the desert
Camels can be seen all over Rajasthan. They are used to carry goods and people, even tourists, for rides into the Sam Dunes. They are animals that are well adapted for the desert because they can go for days without water. They do this by raising their body temperature so that they do not sweat as much. They can also eat the tough desert plants and store fat in their humps and so last for a long time without eating. They have long eyelashes to protect their eyes, and can even keep their eyes shut but still see through their thin eyelids. Camels can also close their nostrils to stop sand getting in.

Tourists are taken for a trek into the desert.

activity sheet 16

Desert life in Rajasthan

1. Look at the map of Rajasthan.
   a. Find the desert.
   b. What is it called?
   c. Colour and label the desert on the map.

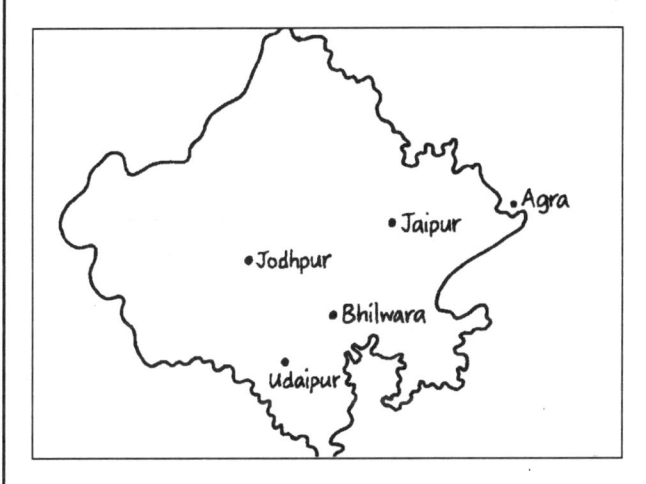

You need
- posters 3—5
- photos 5, 16 and 17
- tourist map of Rajasthan

2. Look at the photograph of the desert on poster 3.
   Describe the features of the desert.

   Plants _____

   _____

   Animals _____

   _____

   Landscape _____

   _____

3. Look at the posters.
   Complete these sentences.

   The women carry water _____

   _____ .

   They leave the village to fetch water

   because _____

   _____ .

4. The water pots are made from gourds.

   These are _____ .

   a. Describe the clothes worn by women.

   _____

   _____

   _____

   _____

   _____

   _____

   _____

   b. Why is the material thin?

   _____

   _____

   _____

5. Why do you think many people are moving from the desert to cities and towns like Jodhpur?

   _____

   _____

   _____

   _____

   _____

© Folens (copiable page)   FOLENS GEOGRAPHY: *An Indian Locality*   47

activity sheet 17

Protecting the environment

You need
- information sheet 6

? Problems

The problem of the increasing desert has been a worry for the Indian government. There are many other environmental problems in India. Forests are being destroyed for mining. Three-quarters of wood cut down in India is used for fuel. So much has disappeared that in some areas women spend all their day trying to find enough wood to cook their families' meals.

When trees are chopped down there are no roots to bind the soil together. The heavy monsoon rains wash it away into the rivers. These rivers then flood causing more damage to farm land and homes.

Forest clearance, changes to the land and the fact that India's population is growing so quickly have also caused problems for India's wildlife. In 1900 there were about 100 000 tigers. Today there are between 4000 and 7200 left.

A tiger.

✔ Solutions

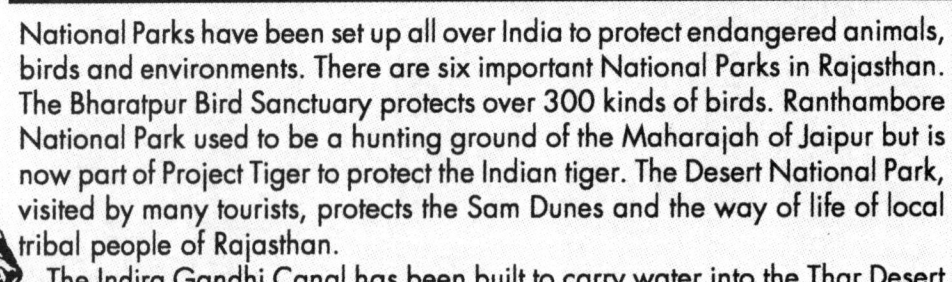

National Parks have been set up all over India to protect endangered animals, birds and environments. There are six important National Parks in Rajasthan. The Bharatpur Bird Sanctuary protects over 300 kinds of birds. Ranthambore National Park used to be a hunting ground of the Maharajah of Jaipur but is now part of Project Tiger to protect the Indian tiger. The Desert National Park, visited by many tourists, protects the Sam Dunes and the way of life of local tribal people of Rajasthan.

The Indira Gandhi Canal has been built to carry water into the Thar Desert which helps the farmers.

Education is being increased for the population of India – and information about farming is important in schools. People are being taught about India's problems and about looking after their environment.

A golden jackal.

1. Plot the deserts of the world on a world map. Where are the hot deserts? Where are the cold deserts?
2. Find out about different sand dunes in other parts of the world. Experiment with trays of sand – try blowing different patterns to see which you can make.
3. Experiment with small pools of water on sand, on different types of soil and different surfaces. When does the water evaporate more quickly? Why?
4. Research animals like the camel that inhabit desert areas. What types of reptiles and birds live in desert places? How are they suited to their environment?
5. National Parks are also important in the UK. Find out where they are and why they have been set up.

Hot deserts	Cold deserts

FOLENS GEOGRAPHY: *An Indian Locality* © Folens (copiable page)

activity sheet 18

Tourism

Tourism is becoming more important to India. Visitors bring money into the country and provide jobs.

Here is a graph which shows how many people visit India in one year, and where they come from. (It does not include visitors from Pakistan and Bangladesh, the countries next to India.)

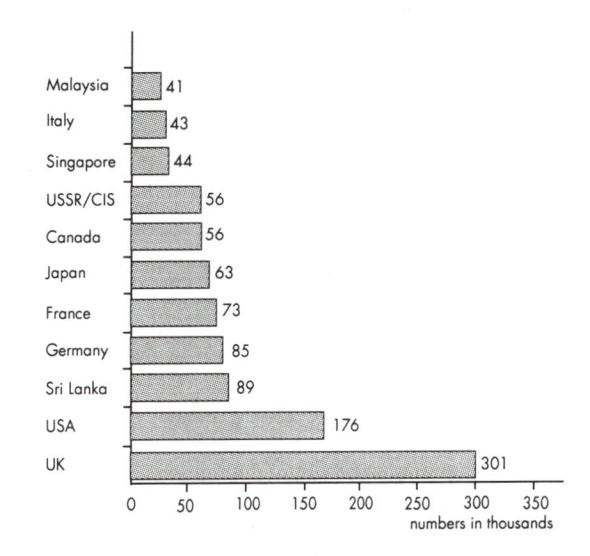

Country	Numbers (thousands)
Malaysia	41
Italy	43
Singapore	44
USSR/CIS	56
Canada	56
Japan	63
France	73
Germany	85
Sri Lanka	89
USA	176
UK	301

Here are some different views about tourism:

"I have got a job in a new hotel. I can earn money to send to my family in the village where they live."

"I can make money by selling food to the visitors, especially during the festivals."

"I am a pilgrim to the holy lake. Five years ago there were only a few hotels. Now there are over 100 and they are spoiling the holiness of the lake."

"We come here to see the beautiful palaces and because the people are so friendly."

"I can't sell the things I make any more. Factories in Delhi are making them cheaper for tourists."

"I'm a tour guide. We try to sell a package tour and take the tourists to all the sights. That way we earn more money."

Activities

1. List reasons why more tourists might cause problems for local people. Try to add some of your own.

2. What are the benefits (good things) of tourism for a town like Jodhpur?

3. Why do so many people visit India? Make a list and add some reasons of your own.

4. Look at the graph. Do most visitors to India come from the West (America and Europe) or from Asian and eastern countries? Can you suggest a reason for this?

5. The UK, USA, Sri Lanka, Canada, Singapore and Malaysia all have large ethnic Indian populations. How does this affect tourism?

© Folens (copiable page) FOLENS GEOGRAPHY: An Indian Locality

An introduction to Jodhpur

History
Jodhpur was one of the greatest Rajput states. The royal family (the Rathores) claimed descent from the Hindu god, Rama, who was the hero of the *Ramayana*. When the kingdom fell, in 1193, the Rathores moved north to Uttar Pradesh, and then into the Thar Desert. They made Mandore the capital of the state in 1381. In the fifteenth century the capital was moved to Jodhpur by Rao Jodha, who founded the old city and started the building of the fort (Meherangarh). Legend says he was advised by a holy man to choose this site. It was built on a rocky outcrop above the flat plains, giving a view of over 120km and was guarded by seven gates. It is said that the architect was buried alive in the fort to keep the design a secret. Rao Jodha then made peace with the Mughals and the head of the family was given the title Maharaja. In 1947 the state became part of India.

[handwritten note: Mention building of the fort. - show pics. How Jodhpur got its name. Jodhpur today. When children look at maps - explain old Jodhpur inside city walls. Have them locate on map. Mention interesting places & locate on map.]

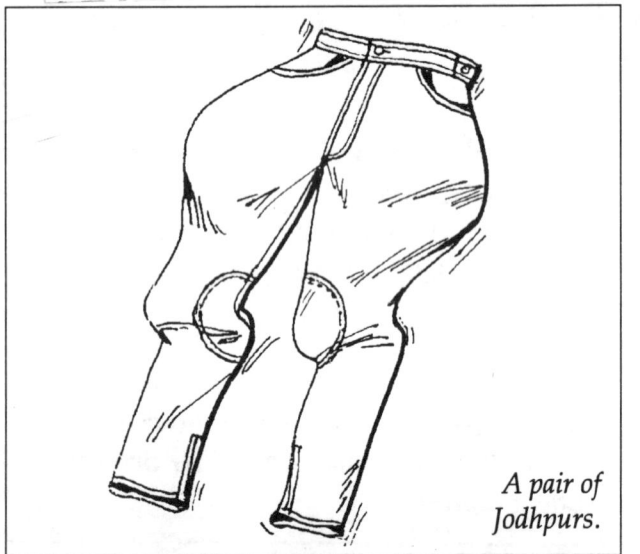

A pair of Jodhpurs.

'Jodhpurs'
Jodhpur is famous for its baggy riding trousers. These were introduced to the British cavalry during World War 1 by Maharaja Pratap Singh who was a commander of the mounted lancers regiment. He lost his luggage during the sea voyage to England and so gave instructions to his tailor on how to make these trousers. Needing a name to put in the order book, the tailor was given the name Jodhpuri and so the fashion was started.

Jodhpur today
Today Jodhpur has a population of 320 000 and is the second largest city in Rajasthan. It is still the area's main trading centre for cattle, camels, cotton, salt, hides and agricultural crops.

Old Jodhpur is inside the old city walls where the buildings were, and still are, painted blue. This used to be the sign that the people of the Brahmin caste lived there, but nowadays most houses are blue because of its cooling and insect repelling properties (there is indigo in the paint). Roofs, however, are kept white to reflect the sun. Modern Jodhpur spreads out from the city walls.

Places of interest
Meherangarh Fort was founded in the fifteenth century and is one of the best preserved forts in Rajasthan. It is made of local sandstone, with ten kilometres of walls, some of which are 45 metres high. There are several impressive gateways, and by the last gate, Lower Pol (Iron Gate) sati handprints can be seen, made by Hindu wives who burned themselves on their husbands' funeral pyres. The palace inside the fort was finished in 1853 and is full of many treasures. Jaswant Thada is a royal cremation ground just inside the old city walls.

Sardar Market bazaar is in the centre of the old town, at the foot of the cliff. It is an open-air market selling fruit, vegetables, spices, trinkets and so on. In the streets around the market are former palaces and temples and traditional craftsmen at work. Jodhpur is especially famous for its puppet makers.

Umaid Bhavan Palace was designed by the British architect, HV Lanchester, and was built by 3000 builders and craftsmen. It is the top hotel in Jodhpur and members of the royal family still live there.

activity sheet 19

The streets of Jodhpur

Jodhpur is a very busy town, with a mixture of markets, bazaars and shops, ancient and modern buildings.

You need
- poster 4
- photos 16–20

- Write an account of street life in Jodhpur. You should include at least a paragraph on each theme on this page.

Shopping

Street sellers:
- What foods are being sold?
- What other items are being sold?
- Why are flowers sold outside shrines?

Shops:
There are also streets of shops similar to the ones in Britian.
- What things can you see being sold by these types of shops?
- How many things can you see being sold by local shops?

Interesting information
- Notice that many of the stalls are vegetable stalls.
- Many Hindus are vegetarian.
- Meat is hard to keep fresh in hot places like Jodhpur.
- When meat is eaten it is usually fish, lamb or chicken.

Transport

- Describe the road surfaces of the Jodhpur streets. Why do you think they are different to the ones we use?
- Describe the different types of transport that are needed.
- Compare street life in Jodhpur with street life in your locality. Which things are the same, which things are different?

Interesting information
Notice the number of bicycles.
- They are the most-used type of transport after walking. Making bicycles is an important industry in India (8 907 240 per year!). The bikes have an older design – the tyres and front forks are made much stronger because of the rough roads and paths.
- Bikes are cheap and don't need expensive roads.

Working animals

- What animals can you see in the streets?
- What jobs are the animals doing?
- Describe the advantages and disadvantages of working animals in the streets.

© Folens (copiable page) FOLENS GEOGRAPHY: *An Indian Locality* 51

A map of Jodhpur

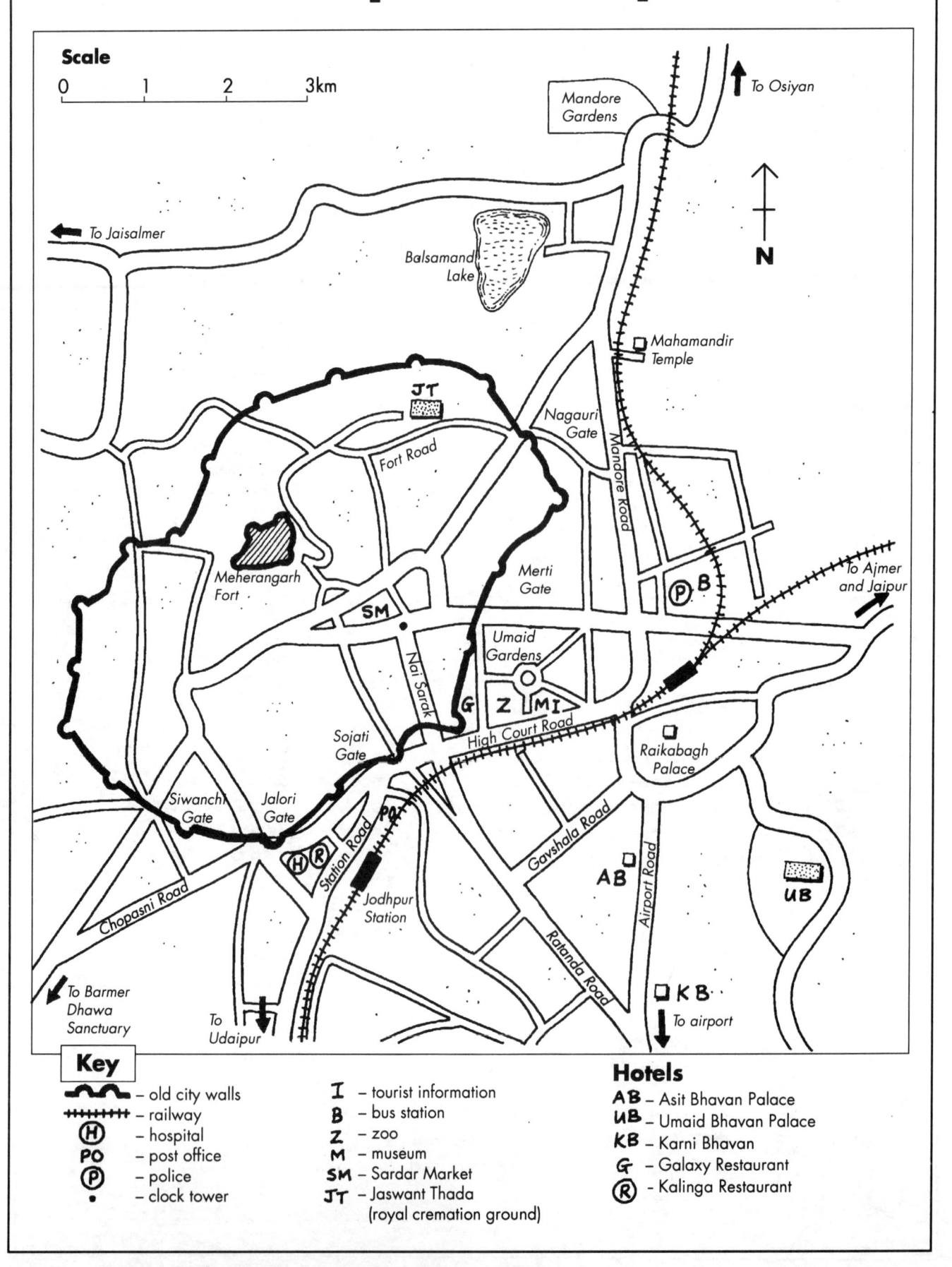

Scale: 0 — 1 — 2 — 3km

N

To Osiyan
To Jaisalmer
Mandore Gardens
Balsamand Lake
Mahamandir Temple
JT
Fort Road
Nagauri Gate
Meherangarh Fort
Merti Gate
SM
Mandore Road
P B
To Ajmer and Jaipur
Nai Sarak
Umaid Gardens
G Z M I
Sojati Gate
High Court Road
Raikabagh Palace
Siwanchi Gate
Jalori Gate
H R
Station Road
PO
Jodhpur Station
Chopasni Road
Gavshala Road
AB
Airport Road
UB
Ratanda Road
KB
To Barmer Dhawa Sanctuary
To Udaipur
To airport

Key

- 〰〰 — old city walls
- ┼┼┼┼ — railway
- Ⓗ — hospital
- PO — post office
- Ⓟ — police
- • — clock tower
- I — tourist information
- B — bus station
- Z — zoo
- M — museum
- SM — Sardar Market
- JT — Jaswant Thada (royal cremation ground)

Hotels

- AB — Asit Bhavan Palace
- UB — Umaid Bhavan Palace
- KB — Karni Bhavan
- G — Galaxy Restaurant
- Ⓡ — Kalinga Restaurant

FOLENS GEOGRAPHY: *An Indian Locality*

activity sheet 20

Finding your way around Jodhpur

The map shows how modern Jodhpur has spread outside the old city walls.

You need
- maps 4 & 5
- poster 4

1. Are these places inside or outside the old city?

   Meherangarh Fort _____   Mahamandir Temple _____

   Sardar Market _____   The police station _____

   The railway station _____

2. You are staying at the Asit Bhavan Palace Hotel. Use the scale bar to calculate how far it is to visit these places. Would you walk, use a rickshaw or a taxi?

Place	Distance (km)	Walk, rickshaw, taxi
Meherangarh Fort		
Umaid Gardens		
Raikabagh Palace		
Sardar Market		
Balsamand Lake		
Kalinga Restaurant		

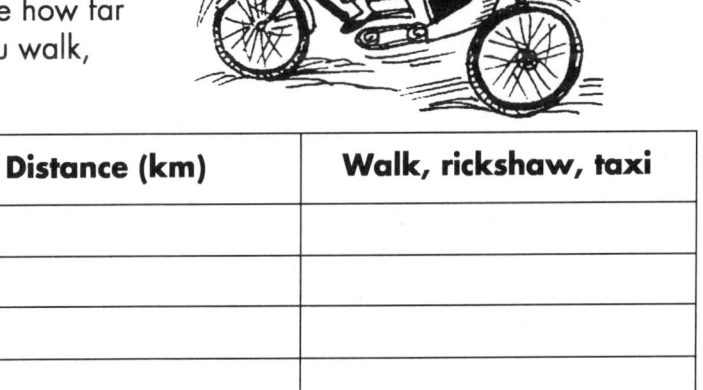

3. You decide to take a walk round the old city walls, starting at the Merti Gate. Describe what you would see from the walls on your walk.

   Walking south from Merti Gate I walk past the Umaid Gardens. In the distance I can see Raikabagh Palace.
   _____
   _____
   _____
   _____

4. Which places could you travel to by train from Jodhpur station?
   _____   _____   _____

5. Give clear directions to someone walking from Jodhpur railway station to the Asit Bhavan Palace Hotel.
   _____
   _____
   _____

© Folens (copiable page)   FOLENS GEOGRAPHY: *An Indian Locality*

activity sheet 21

Origins of Jodhpur

Special maps called relief maps are sometimes used to show the shape of the land or what the landscape is like in a particular place. These maps show the shape of the land and the height of the land, either by colours or shading or by using contour lines.

Here is a drawing of contour lines which shows the shape of the hill of Meherangarh Fort in Jodhpur.

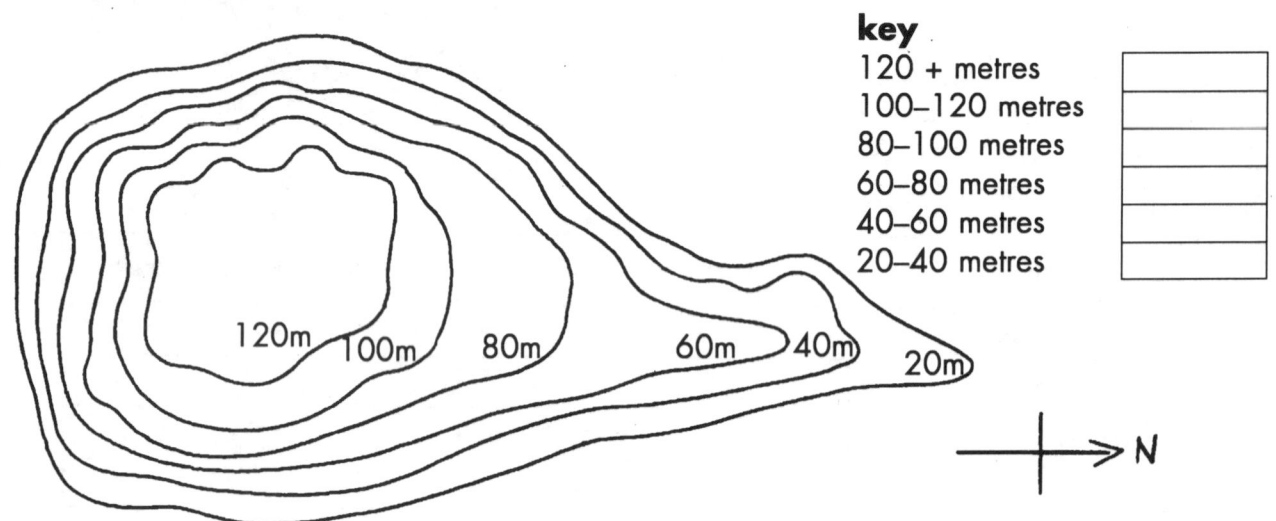

key
120 + metres
100–120 metres
80–100 metres
60–80 metres
40–60 metres
20–40 metres

1. The fort is 120 metres above the flat desert valley.
   Colour the land:
   above 120 metres – dark brown
   between 100 and 120 metres – light brown
   between 80 and 100 metres – red
   between 60 and 80 metres – orange
   between 40 and 60 metres – green
   between 20 and 40 metres – leave white.

2. Now colour the key.

3. Label three points where the slope is steep: S.

4. Label two points where the slope is gentle: G.

5. Mark a point where you think the main gate is: gate.

6. The fort, around which Jodhpur has grown, was built in 1453. Many other forts such as Udaipur and Jaipur were built in a similar way.

   Explain why you think forts were built on hills and with strong walls in this way.

   _____
   _____
   _____
   _____
   _____
   _____

FOLENS GEOGRAPHY: *An Indian Locality*

activity sheet 22

Meherangarh Fort

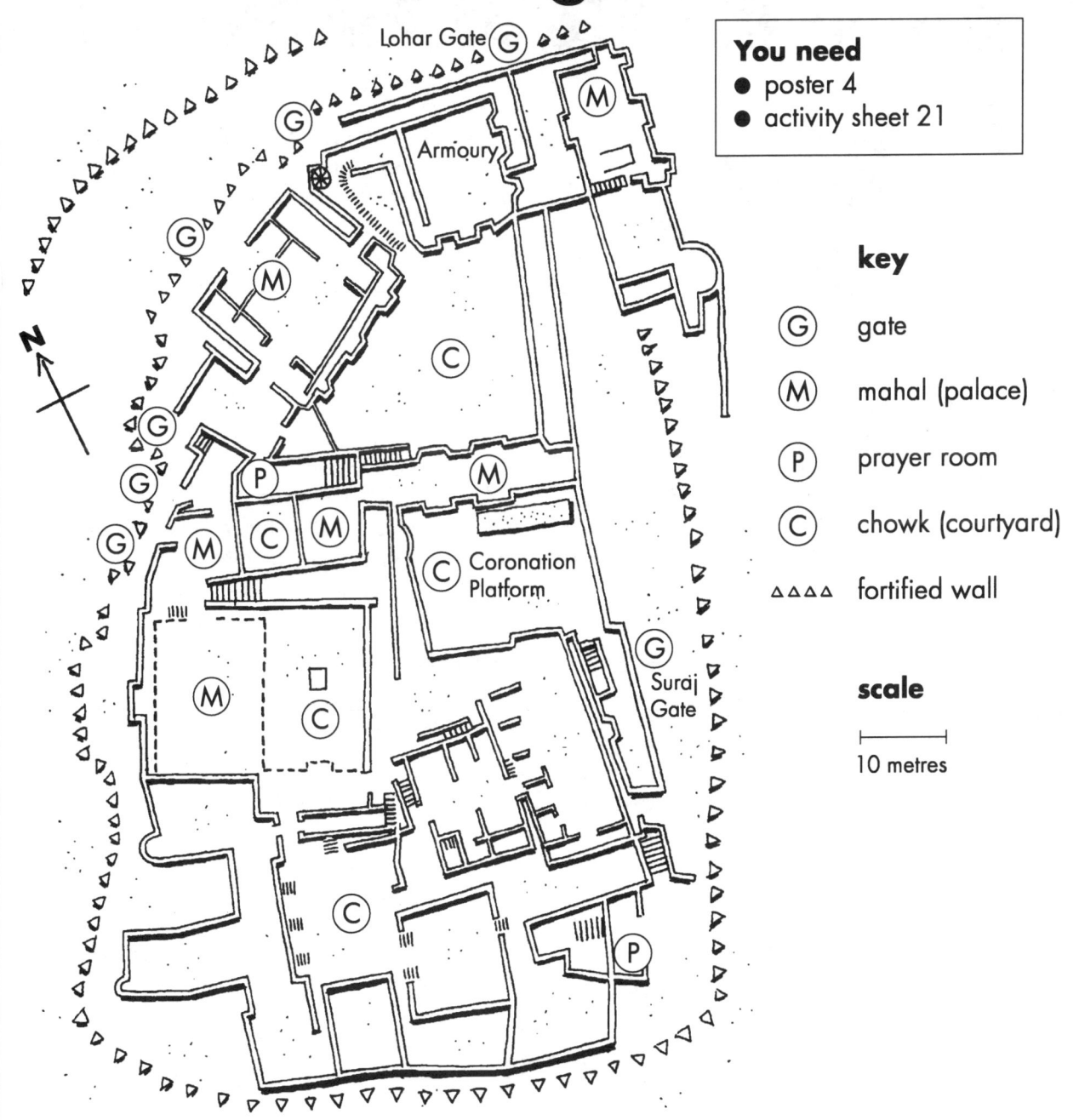

You need
- poster 4
- activity sheet 21

key
- G gate
- M mahal (palace)
- P prayer room
- C chowk (courtyard)
- ▵▵▵▵ fortified wall

scale

⊢———⊣
10 metres

This is a plan of the Meherangarh Fort at Jodhpur.

1. How many gates were there into the fort?
2. Look at the photograph on the poster and your relief map. Why do you think there were no gates on the southern side?
3. Which do you think was the most important courtyard? Why do you think it was important?
4. What is the approximate length and width of the fort?
5. What is the approximate perimeter of the fortified wall?
6. Why do you think the fort was built on a hill like this?
7. Suraj means sun. Why do you think Suraj Gate was given this name?

© Folens (copiable page)   FOLENS GEOGRAPHY: An Indian Locality   55

pupil information sheet 7

A day in the life of TulsiRam Jat

Here I am at school with some of my friends.

Hello, I am TulsiRam. I am 12 years old and live in Jodhpur. I am Hindu, and my god is Durga. I speak Mewari and Hindi. I am vegetarian.

My home is really in a village 90km away where the rest of my family live. I have two older brothers and a sister. It takes about three hours by bus to get home and I have just been home for the festival of Raksha Bandhan.

I have come to Jodhpur to work as a house boy for Renuka and Bawaji, cleaning, sweeping, cooking and gardening, and have lived here for nearly two years. My mother is ill with cancer so cannot look after me, but I see her every month and my new family cares for me. I have my own room.

Here is a diary of one of my days:

Morning

6.30am I wake up, wash and make tea for Bawaji and Renuka.
7.30am Breakfast – usually bread, butter and milk.
7.45am I go to the shop for eggs and bread.
7.55am I wash up.
8am I start sweeping, mopping and dusting.
8.30am I go into the garden to get flowers for our shrine. Then I finish cleaning and wash the bathroom.
9.30am I get breakfast for Renuka and Bawaji – usually eggs, toast and tea.
11.30am I have a bath.
11.45am I get ready for school.
12.15pm I set off to school. I am in the second standard and I have only been at school for one year because I did not go to school in my village.

Afternoon

12.30–5pm I am at school. My favourite lessons are studying Hindi and drawing.
5.15pm I am home from school and change out of my school clothes.
5.30pm I water the plants, get my clothes from the line and iron them.
6–8pm This is my own time. I usually play with my cars or work in the garden. I have my own patch where I grow squash, green chillies, tomatoes, cucumbers and gourds. I have also planted some orange and melon seeds but they haven't grown yet. In my village we have a farm and we grow lots of things. Sometimes I sit and draw.
8pm I go to get the milk from the milkman.
8.15pm I have my supper – usually roti, dhal and vegetables.
8.30–9pm I am allowed to watch TV.
9–9.45pm I do my homework.
10pm I go to bed.

pupil information sheet 8

Children in Jodhpur

Not all the children in Jodhpur have lives like TulsiRam. Even though the law has tried to change society in India, there are still different 'castes' of people, which affects how and where people live. Virendra is a Rajput – one of the highest, and oldest castes in India.

"Hello, I am Virendra Singh Shaktawat. I am a Hindu and a Rajput and go to private school. I have one younger brother called Nitu. Here is a diary of one of my days":

I wake up at 6am and have a bath, then I get dressed in my school uniform. I have breakfast at 7am, usually eggs.

I leave for school at 7.10am and walk there because it isn't far. School starts at 7.30am. We have four lessons until 11.30am, 30 minutes' lunch break, then four more lessons after lunch. We finish school at 1.35pm.

My favourite subject is science, and my worst is maths. When I get home I usually have something to eat and then watch TV for an hour. I do my homework next, until 5pm.

After tea I go out to play with my special friend, Junjeet. We like to play football, go horse riding or roller-skating. Sometimes I go up to Sweetie's roof (she's my cousin) and roller-skate.

At 8pm I have my evening meal and then watch TV until bedtime. I usually go to bed at 10pm. I like to watch movies – especially those with lots of fighting.

I get up at 8am and study until 9am. I have my breakfast, then study again until 11am. Then I have a bath and get ready for school.

I leave for school at about 12.10pm and walk because it is not far to go. School starts at 12.30pm. We work until 3pm, then have a break for lunch. We have four lessons in this time. After lunch we have four more lessons until 5.30pm.

The subjects we study are English, maths, Hindi, social studies, social science, arts and crafts, moral science, health education and Sanskrit. My best subjects are science and social studies. My worst subject is drawing.

After school I walk home and get changed. I have my evening meal at 6pm, then I go and play in the park with my friends for an hour. After that I do my homework until 8.30pm. I watch TV until bedtime, which is 10pm.

My favourite hobby is watching Hindi movies. When I grow up I want to be a doctor, that's why I work hard with my studies.

"Hello, I am Payal Chandwani and I am ten years old. I came originally from Sindh. I have one younger brother called Paresh. Here is some information about my day:"

© Folens (copiable page)   FOLENS GEOGRAPHY: *An Indian Locality*   57

activity sheet 23

At school in Jodhpur

You need
● photos 6–8

Here is a timetable of the school week from TulsiRam's school in Jodhpur.

		12.45–1.15	1.15–1.45	1.45–2.15	2.15–2.45		3.00–3.30	3.30–4.00	4.00–4.30	4.30–5.00
Mon	assembly and registration	social studies	social science	Hindi	Hindi	break	maths	maths	arts and crafts	individual work
Tues		social studies	social science	Hindi	Hindi		maths	maths	arts and crafts	individual work
Wed		social studies	social science	Hindi	Hindi		maths	maths	arts and crafts	individual work
Thurs		social studies	social science	Hindi	Hindi		maths	maths	arts and crafts	individual work
Fri		PE	PE	Hindi	Hindi		maths	moral science	arts and crafts	individual work
Sat		social studies	social science	Hindi	Hindi		maths	moral science	arts and crafts	individual work

1. Work out how much time is spent on different subjects by TulsiRam. Compare this to the amount of time you spend in a school week on your subjects.
   How do they compare?
   Are any subjects missing, different, the same?

2. Look closely at the photographs of school life in Jodhpur and this timetable. Write some sentences about similarities and differences between the school and your own school like this:

   Differences

   The children are working outside.

   Similarities

   The children are having an assembly.

3. Discuss with a small group then write your thoughts about TulsiRam's day.
   ● What do you think about him working away from home?
   ● What are the benefits for him of leaving his village?
   ● How would you feel about leaving home at 12 years old and working part-time?

4. Write a diary for one of your school days, as TulsiRam did. How much time do you spend at school, helping with jobs at home, watching TV, and on hobbies? Compare your day with TulsiRam's – do you think your day is harder or easier?

Teachers' notes (mask before photocopying)
The children will need to be given some background information about Hinduism so that they can understand more about TulsiRam's life. Use this page alongside page 57 about two other children in Jodhpur to show the differences within Jodhpur.

FOLENS GEOGRAPHY: *An Indian Locality* © Folens (copiable page)

pupil information sheet 9

Living in Jodhpur

Here is Vardhi Bai; she is 68 years old. She is Hindu and speaks Mewari. She is married with a married son and daughter who live away from home. She has eight grandchildren.

Here is a typical day for Vardhi:

I get up at 5am and go out to the toilet – we don't have one in my house. Then I collect buckets of water from the well to fill my bath.

6am I do my mala (like a rosary) for about 15 minutes. Then I sweep and clean the house. I wash the pots and polish them with ash before refilling them with water.

7am I make tea. I prepare vegetables, chop and peel then cook them. I make the dough ready for the chapattis.
After cooking, I give my husband his breakfast – vegetables or a paratha. I pack up his tiffin (lunch box) with vegetables that are left, chapattis and home-made pickles.

8.30am My husband goes to work – he works in upholstery. Then I wash the kitchen floor and have my bath.

10am I go to the temple; I go every day, and on the way back I buy vegetables and any thread I need for my sewing.

11am I have my lunch and then I sleep until about

12.30pm. Sometimes I go to visit my brother or sister.

2–5pm I do my sewing work. When I was younger I used to work longer hours but now I just do three hours a day. Lots of people bring me their clothes for stitching.

5pm I chat for a while to the neighbours and then I go in to prepare the evening meal.

6.30pm My husband comes home from work and we have our evening meal. After dinner I wash up. By now I am feeling very tired.

9.30pm I go to sleep.

I have made lots of journeys from my home. I have been to all four holy places where the Kumbh Mela (our Hindu festival) is held: Ujain, Haridwar, Nasik and Prayag. I have also been to Puri, Badrinath, Rameswaram, Somnath and Girna. I usually travel by bus or train.

Now I am just waiting to go up to heaven.

Teachers' notes (mask before photocopying)
Mewari is one of the two dialects of Rajasthani.
There is a huge pantheon of gods in Hinduism. Vardhi's special gods are Mataji and Asha Pura, who are two of the main folk deities of Rajasthan. Other than farming, industries associated with cotton and materials are one of the biggest employers – see page 34.

© Folens (copiable page)   FOLENS GEOGRAPHY: *An Indian Locality*

Living in Jodhpur

Activities

The children will need to use:
- information sheets 7, 8 and 9
- posters 3 and 4
- A4 photos.

Virendra is a Rajput. The children can compare his day with that of TulsiRam. They can discuss what effect being of a 'higher caste' has had on Virendra's life.

Many children in India, especially in the villages, are not as lucky as TulsiRam. Looking carefully at the photographs of children on the posters, the children can try to imagine and describe a day in the life of one of these children.

The children can research the caste system and then discuss its consequences. They can debate recent laws trying to end the caste system.

The children can discuss poverty in economically developing areas – especially in areas such as Rajasthan. List problems caused for individuals, families, the country itself and then suggest solutions. Is world aid the only answer? Discuss the increase in industrialisation, especially in Rajasthan, such as cement works.

Discuss Vardhi's day. Ask the children to interview their grandparents and make diaries of their days to compare with Vardhi's. Can their grandparents provide insights into their days when they were young? Has life become easier or harder for them?

In many areas of India the 'extended family' is still very strong. Who looks after the children's grandparents? What do they think about the lives of old people in the UK? In India?

The children can look at the diaries and compare them with their own diary of activities. How are these activities affected by the locality in which they live?

For example:
- the weather
- religious customs
- family life
- social customs
- health and sanitation.

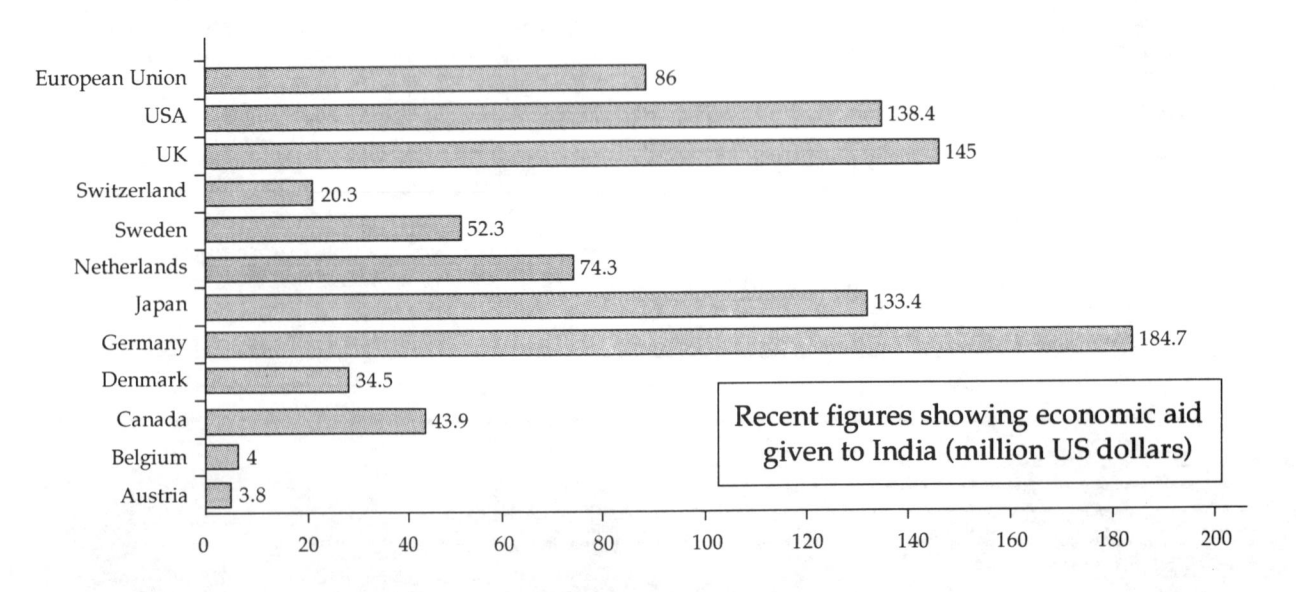

Children can discuss similarities between free time activities.

Country	Aid (million US dollars)
European Union	86
USA	138.4
UK	145
Switzerland	20.3
Sweden	52.3
Netherlands	74.3
Japan	133.4
Germany	184.7
Denmark	34.5
Canada	43.9
Belgium	4
Austria	3.8

Recent figures showing economic aid given to India (million US dollars)

activity sheet 24

The puppet makers of Jodhpur

There are many different kinds of craftsmen working in Jodhpur. The puppet makers are famous all over India. They act out old stories of heroes and legends using their puppets, something which has gone on for hundreds of years. The puppet is called a 'kathputli', the puppeteer a 'kathputliwala'. The puppets are usually one metre tall, and are operated with two strings. They have carved heads made of wood and wear fancy costumes.

Shadow puppets are also an old tradition in India. These are flat puppets, richly carved, and worked by rods. They are usually made of leather and are sometimes dyed. They are held against the back of a screen, with a light shining from behind them to make shadows on the screen, and the audience watches from the front. Most plays have been based on the story of Rama and his victory over the ten-headed demon, Ravanna. Sometimes, when these plays are shown in front of Bhadraki temples today, they can last for three weeks.

An Indian puppet show

Work with a group to make Jodhpur puppets using modelling clay or balsa wood and brightly coloured materials. You can also make shadow puppets from cardboard, using small garden canes or dowels as rods. Make shadows on a large screen using an overhead projector.
You will need to research an old Indian legend, Hindu story or write your own story.

© Folens (copiable page)   FOLENS GEOGRAPHY: *An Indian Locality*

Reviewing the topic

Concept maps

Concept maps are a useful way of reviewing the issues raised in the study of this locality.

Opposite is a page of images to be used by the children as starting points in this process.

- What change can children see taking place in Rajasthan – in buildings, transport, work, farming methods, where people live and work and so on?

Children can link the pictures in any way they think is relevant, and of course add their own drawings.

Captions are added under the drawings. Then the children explain why they have chosen to link certain images.

Images can have more than one link.

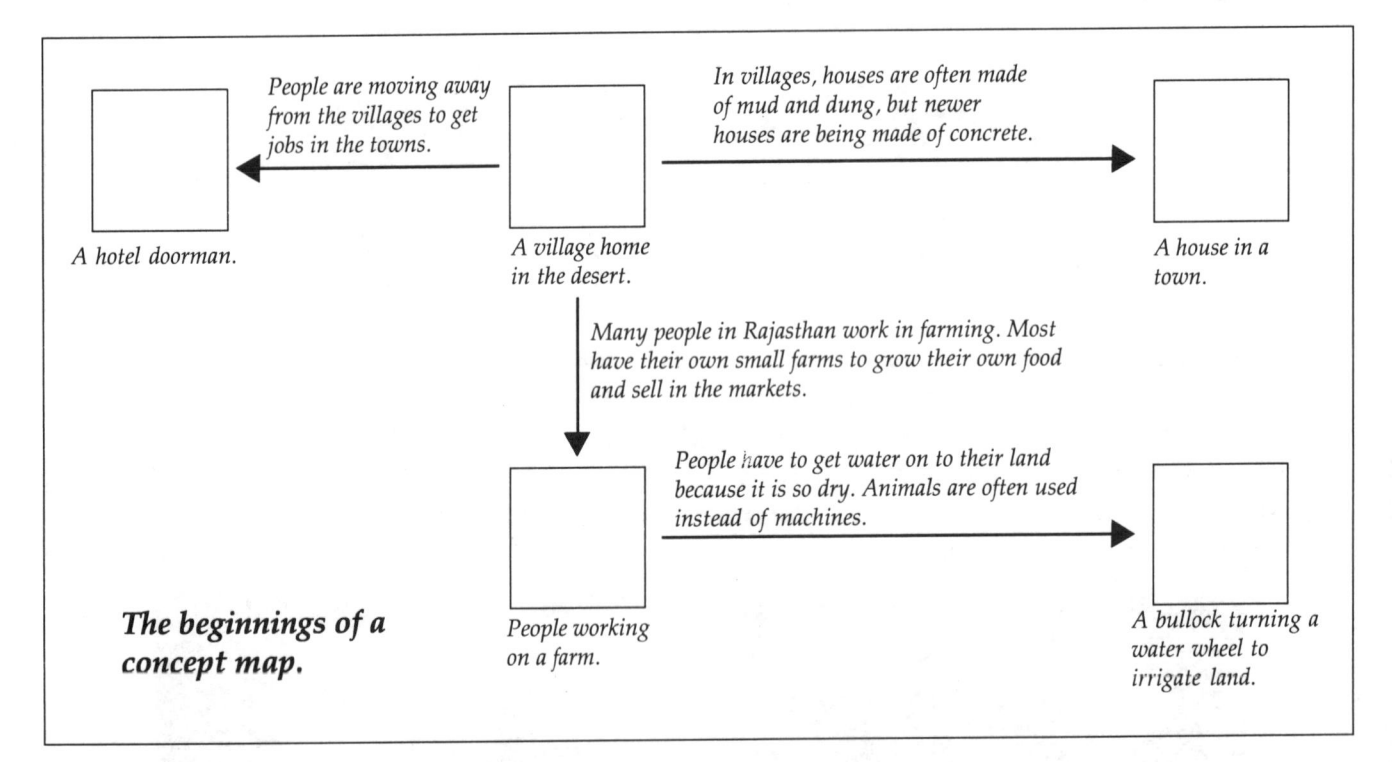

The beginnings of a concept map.

- [A hotel doorman.] ← *People are moving away from the villages to get jobs in the towns.* — [A village home in the desert.] — *In villages, houses are often made of mud and dung, but newer houses are being made of concrete.* → [A house in a town.]

- [A village home in the desert.] ↓ *Many people in Rajasthan work in farming. Most have their own small farms to grow their own food and sell in the markets.* → [People working on a farm.] — *People have to get water on to their land because it is so dry. Animals are often used instead of machines.* → [A bullock turning a water wheel to irrigate land.]

The children's concept maps can be used to help with assessment of what the children have learned and understood, and can also be used for assessment of the teaching and future planning – if certain elements do not appear on the children's maps then perhaps the emphasis of your work needs altering!

Prompt words can be given for some children which give clues of the important issues.

Questions to consider first or to look for in assessment might be:

- What do the images show? Can children describe features of Rajasthan – physical, the people, clothes, work and so on?

- What things do not appear to be changing?

- How does the landscape affect the people? What do the children think it would be like to live in the Thar Desert?

- How does the weather affect the people? What would it be like to go to school in a monsoon? How do people grow food?

- Why have Jodhpur and other towns grown where they have?

- Why is India still a developing country? Can people do anything to 'improve' their way of life?

FOLENS GEOGRAPHY: *An Indian Locality*

FOLENS GEOGRAPHY: *An Indian Locality*

Something to cook

Here is a small collection of traditional Rajasthani recipes for things which can easily be made in school.

PAKORA

Ingredients
1kg garam flour
1 bunch fresh spinach
1kg potatoes
1 large onion
8 teaspoons red chilli powder
5 teaspoons of salt
Some coriander (fresh or ground)
2 teaspoons of garam masala spice

Method
Peel the potatoes, wash and cut into small slices.
Chop the onions, spinach and coriander into small pieces.
Mix all these together in a bowl.
Add the garam flour and mix.
Mix in the chilli powder, garam masala and salt.
While heating the oil, add a little water to the mixture until it is thin.
When the oil is hot, add a tablespoon of the mixture and fry until brown. Continue adding tablespoons of the mixture to cook.
Eat hot or cold.

VEGETABLE KEBABS

Ingredients
100g cauliflower
100g peas
100g spinach
100g rice (basmati)
100g garam flour
1 teaspoon of baking powder
3 green chillies
3 small potatoes
100g coriander
1 teaspoon of salt

Method
Mix all the ingredients, except the coriander, in a grinder.
When it is fully mashed, add the coriander.
Make the mixture into small burgers.
Fry them in oil until golden brown.
Eat hot.

APPLE KHEER

Ingredients
1 litre of milk
4 tablespoons of sugar
3 medium dessert apples, cored and peeled
1 level teaspoon of cardamon powder
3 almonds, blanched and sliced

Method
Put the milk on to boil, add the sugar and cook gently until the mixture is reduced by half.
Grate the apples and add to the milk.
Bring to the boil; remove from heat.
Sprinkle cardamons and almonds on top.
Serve hot.

MAKKI KI FIMI

Ingredients
500g fresh corn kernels
250g sugar
11g powdered cardamon seeds
1 litre milk
115g cream

Method
Grate the corn kernels; grind finely.
Add milk, sugar and cardamon; stir well.
Cook on low heat, stirring constantly to avoid lumps.
When thick, remove from heat and leave to cool.
Add cream and stir well.
Serve cold.

CHAPATIS

Ingredients
675g wholemeal flour
4 tablespoons of plain flour
ghee or butter for serving

Method
Mix wholemeal flour with water to make a dough.
Leave for 30 minutes.
Knead again.
Pull off pieces the size of ping-pong balls.
Dip in plain flour.
Flatten out with a rolling pin.
Heat a griddle (or heavy frying pan).
Cook for 15–20 seconds on each side.